CLASSIC
DEEM SUM

Yukiko and Bob Haydock

JAPANESE GARNISHES

MORE JAPANESE GARNISHES

ORIENTAL APPETIZERS

HENRY CHAN
YUKIKO AND BOB HAYDOCK

CLASSIC DEEM SUM

HOLT, RINEHART AND WINSTON · NEW YORK

Copyright © 1985 by Yukiko and Bob Haydock
All rights reserved, including the right to reproduce
this book or portions thereof in any form.
Published by Holt, Rinehart and Winston,
383 Madison Avenue, New York, New York 10017.
Published simultaneously in Canada by Holt, Rinehart
and Winston of Canada, Limited.

Library of Congress Cataloging in Publication Data
Chan, Henry.
Classic deem sum.
1. Dim sum. 2. Snack foods. 3. Cookery,
Chinese. I. Haydock, Yukiko. II. Haydock,
Bob. III. Title.
TX724.5.C5C455 1985   641.8   85–806
ISBN 0–03–071546–6

First Edition

Designed by Amy Hill
Printed in the United States of America
10 9 8 7 6 5 4 3 2 1

ISBN 0-03-071546-6

To my late, beloved mother, from whose
love of life and food all else flowed.
—HC

CONTENTS

INTRODUCTION   1

INGREDIENTS   3

TECHNIQUES AND TOOLS   9

STEAMED DISHES

CHICKEN CRESCENTS   **20**
Gai nup fun gwor

BEEF BASKETS   **22**
Gnow yuk shiu mye

FOUR COLOR DUMPLINGS   **24**
Say sik shiu mye

SHRIMP MOONS   **26**
Har gow

BARBECUED PORK BUNS   **28**
Char shiu bow

BEEF AND WATERCRESS   **30**
Sai choy ngow yuk

STEAMED SPARERIBS   **32**
See jup pai gwut

MANDARIN DUMPLINGS   **34**
Saam ling gow

RICE NOODLE ROLLS   **36**
Cheung fun

STEAMED PEARL BALLS   **38**
Jun jew kao

LOTUS LEAF RICE   **40**
Naw mai gai

SHRIMP GOLDFISH   **44**
Gum yue gow

DEEP-FRIED DISHES

SHRIMP TOAST   **48**
Har dor see

CHICKEN LOLLIPOPS   **50**
Yeung gai yik

SPRING ROLLS   **52**
Cheun guen

TARO DUMPLINGS   **56**
Woo gok

SWEET RICE DUMPLINGS   **58**
Haam suey gok

BEAN CURD SKIN ROLLS   **60**
San juk guen

FRIED FISH BALLS   **64**
Jar yue yuen

SILVER-WRAPPED CHICKEN   **66**
Jee bow gai

CREAM CHEESE WONTON   **68**
"Cheese" Wun tun

STUFFED CRAB CLAWS   **70**
Yeung hai keem

PAN-FRIED DISHES

POT STICKERS   **74**
War teep

TURNIP CAKES   **76**
Law bak go

STUFFED BEAN CURD   **78**
Yeung tofu

ROASTED OR BAKED DISHES

BARBECUED PORK **82**
Char shiu

GOLDEN COIN PORK **84**
Gum cheen gai

BARBECUED SPARERIBS **86**
Shiu pai gwut

CHICKEN TURNOVERS **88**
Gai gok

SWEET DISHES

CUSTARD TARTS **92**
Daan tart

SESAME SEED BALLS **94**
Jeen duey

BLACK SESAME ROLLS **96**
Jee ma guen

DOUGHS

HAR GOW DOUGH **100**
Har gow pay

POT STICKER WRAPPERS **102**
War teep pay

BASIC BUN DOUGH **104**
Bow pay

PASTRY DOUGH **106**
So pay

SWEET RICE DOUGH **108**
Haam suey gok pay

WONTON SKINS **110**
Wun tun pay

OILS, SAUCES, AND STOCK

SZECHUAN PEPPERCORN OIL **114**

CHILI PEPPER OIL **114**

SOY SAUCE–CHILI PEPPER OIL DIP **114**

SOY SAUCE–CHILI PEPPER OIL–VINEGAR DIP **114**

SOY SAUCE–SZECHUAN PEPPERCORN OIL DIP **115**

MUSTARD–SOY SAUCE DIP **115**

SOY SAUCE–SZECHUAN PEPPERCORN OIL–VINEGAR DIP **115**

BEAN CURD SAUCE **115**

CHICKEN STOCK **116**

INDEX **117**

INTRODUCTION

The ancient art of deem sum began seven centuries ago in the palaces of the Sung Dynasty. There, inventive palace chefs learned to pique the jaded royal palates with endless, inventive varieties of bite-size delicacies. When the ruthless thirteenth-century Mongol invasions forced the court to move slowly south toward Guangzhou (Canton), they took their culinary traditions with them.

The deem sum idea spread to each stop on the way, where local cooks devised their own imitations of the rich, imperial tidbits. By 1900 Guangdung Province became the unchallenged leader of China's deem sum tradition. The deem sum journey did not end there, of course, since in a few decades another massive political upheaval was to send others fleeing—many to the United States—carrying with them little aside from their traditions.

Regardless of the setting, East or West, the basic deem sum idea is the same. You feast on a succession of flavorful small treats—steamed, fried, baked, grilled—that emerge from the kitchen in a continuous parade of carts and trays. You sip tea, contemplate the offerings, and wait for messages from your appetite center. A wave of the hand in the direction of a grilled turnip cake, a succulent shrimp-filled dumpling, or perhaps a stuffed chicken wing that has been steamed and then fried to a crispy gold, will cause it to be placed instantly before you. Wise diners will ask for single orders so they may sample more. Still wiser regulars will come early, stay late, and sit close to the swinging kitchen doors to get first crack at the emerging carts. For us indecisive souls who have difficulty selecting from assorted entrées on a Western menu, the teahouse is heaven. You can have it all! When you have sipped your last cup of jasmine, and disposed of your last delectable tea pastry, your bill is totaled simply by counting the empty plates at so much a plate. And off you go, fortune cookie slip in hand: "You will never go hungry."

The art of deem sum is best sampled at first amidst the clatter and friendly bustle of the teahouse or restaurant, where the aroma of freshly made deem sum wafting lightly from the kitchen works its appetizing magic on you. You order shiu mye, har gow, woo gok, yeung gai yik, war teep, or jeen duey with the casual assurance of an old China hand. All you need do is point at what you want.

Restaurants, at their best, let us discover the subtleties and complexities

1

of a foreign cuisine firsthand. In fact, it is through restaurants that a cuisine first develops a foothold in a new land. Later, cookbooks, magazines and classes will fill the need to learn more about new foods, but in the beginning it is the restaurant that captures our interest and keeps the tastes alive.

Often, the restaurant trade is the only one by which an uprooted family can find itself a place in a new country. Yank Sing restaurant in San Francisco was opened twenty-seven years ago by just such a family.

In 1949, George Chan, a landowner, and his wife, Alice, the youngest daughter of the proprietor of the famous Tai Ping Kwoon Restaurant of Guangzhou (Canton), fled China with their four small children for the relative safety of Hong Kong. After a few years, they left that temporary sanctuary for America where, with the encouragement of friends, they opened their first deem sum restaurant in 1958 in a small shop front on the edge of San Francisco's Chinatown. They called it Yank Sing, an old name for Canton meaning "City of Rams."

The deem sum idea took hold at this latest stop on its journey, as it had so many centuries before, and the San Francisco restaurant flourished. The intervening years have seen several moves to better quarters. Today Yank Sing diners can enjoy one of San Francisco's great luncheon experiences at 427 Battery Street under the attentive supervision of the Chans' son, co-author of this book Henry Chan. The dining here can be as relaxed and pleasurable as you might imagine it was in old Canton when nineteenth-century patrons spent lazy mornings sipping tea, sampling deem sum, and pondering the issues of life with their companions.

The carts keep rolling along, catering to ever growing numbers discovering deem sum for themselves, and setting the stage for the next stop on its westward migration—the home kitchen. The proliferating world of oriental markets is giving all of us access to the ingredients that make preparing deem sum in the home a realistic possibility. So we authors have joined together in the hopeful notion that we can produce a book that can be helpful to those of you who want to try your hand.

The recipes have been selected from Yank Sing's repertoire, and all have been reworked and tested for the home kitchen. The results were returned to Yank Sing for final scrutiny and testing. What has emerged is a collection we believe will work for you. They are varied and exciting possibilities for a different dinner or luncheon, hors d'oeuvres, or even as the perfect picnic. Some recipes will involve an hour or two of work, while others need a day of advance preparation for best results. But whatever the time involved, these tasty treats are worth the effort. Now it is your turn to play a part in culinary history-making. Open your kitchens to deem sum.

——H. C., Y. H., and B. H.

INGREDIENTS

Bamboo Shoots. Fresh bamboo shoots are seldom available in this country, from either domestic or imported sources. But the canned, water-packed variety are plentiful and serve our purposes very well. Wash the shoots after removing them from the can. If you buy a can of whole tips (not already chopped), slice them in half before washing. A sour white residue sometimes collects on the interior sections and should be washed away. Refrigerate leftover shoots in water in a screw top jar. They will keep for about a week with a change of water every two days.

Bean Curd. Bean curd (tofu) is made from soybeans that are first softened in water and then crushed and boiled to produce milk. The residual pulp is strained out and the milk coagulated to form curds, which are then pressed in molds. It is sold in the United States packed in water and sealed in plastic tubs. Buy the Chinese-style "firm" tofu.

Bean Curd (Red). Most Westerners are familiar with tofu, the white fresh curd made from soybeans. Fresh bean curd that has been preserved with salt and spices is sold as preserved or fermented bean curd. It comes in jars or cans and can be either red or white in color. It has the texture of soft cheese and is quite salty.

Bean Curd Skins. Thin sheets of dried bean curd are available in 8- × 14-inch packages in oriental markets. The skins are often used as wrappers for fillings. They must first be soaked to make them pliable, and then cut to the required size.

Bean Sauce (Ground). Bean sauce comes in two forms, ground and whole. The ground bean sauce has a smoother texture but otherwise the two are quite similar, especially in their mutually salty flavor. The sauce is made from fermented soybeans.

Black Beans (Salted). Salted black beans are an intensely flavorful, salty seasoning. Chefs will usually wash away the extreme saltiness by immersing them in water and draining several times. Even so, enough saltiness remains so that we do not recommend adding salt to any recipe using black beans. The beans are sold in sealed plastic or in cans and are often seasoned with ginger.

Black Chinese Mushrooms (Dried). The caps of these dried mushrooms range in diameter from under an inch to about 2½ inches. They range in price depending on the size and texture of the cap. Since all of the deem sum recipes require that the caps be chopped, the cheaper, less attractive varieties may be bought. The mushrooms need to be reconstituted in warm water and the tough stems removed. The Japanese shiitake mushroom is virtually the same product, and may be substituted. The mushrooms will keep for many months if stored in a covered jar in a cool, dark location. We hesitate to recommend sealable plastic bags since once an expensive supply was devoured by mushroom munching bugs that mysteriously managed to get in. If you do use the plastic bags, be sure they are sealed properly.

Chicken Stock. Chicken stock is such an important ingredient in many of these recipes that instructions for making it at home are given in the Oils, Sauces, and Stocks section. Quite simply, chicken parts are simmered for several hours with crushed scallions. The resulting stock is degreased and refrigerated or frozen for future use. This recipe is always used when chicken stock is required in this book. If canned chicken stock is substituted, the results are often too salty unless salt is reduced or eliminated in the main recipe.

Chili Oil. Chili oil can be purchased in oriental stores, or can be made at home by adding scallion and crushed ginger to hot vegetable oil, which is then allowed to cool for five minutes. The scallion and ginger are removed and dried crushed chili is added and allowed to sit overnight. In the morning the finished oil is strained into a clean bottle and stored in the refrigerator. Chili oil is used primarily as a condiment. The residual crushed chilis can be the basis for making a delicious chili pepper sauce.

Chili Peppers. A variety of fresh hot chilis on the market will add fiery flavor to sauces and stuffings. Either the red or green varieties are suitable. They are used whole, finely chopped, or sliced. Normally the seeds (the hottest part) are removed. Take care when handling chilis. The oil can irritate the skin and accidentally be rubbed into the eyes. Wash your hands thoroughly after use.

Chili Pepper Sauce. Chili pepper sauce is a combination of soy sauce, chopped peppers, radishes, garlic, and black beans that have been combined in oil. Several brands are available in oriental food stores. Yank Sing packages a particularly delicious chili pepper sauce in 7-ounce jars under its own name. A dab of chili pepper sauce swirled around in a small dish of soy sauce makes a tangy dip for many deem sums.

Chinese Cabbage. Chinese cabbage is a sweet, mild cabbage that is a joy to eat raw. Other names for it include celery cabbage, napa cabbage, tientsin and pe-tsai (Chinese), and hakusai (Japanese). It grows in an elongated shape somewhat like romaine lettuce, rather than the conventional ball shape. Its color is white at the base and changes to a pale, light green in the leaves, which are tightly wrapped about one another. The head is usually about 8 to 10 inches long.

Chinese Pork Sausage. Chinese pork sausages are usually sold in pairs, joined together with a string. They are slightly sweet, dried, fairly hard to the touch, and dotted with imbedded clumps of pork fat. They are generally about 6 to 8 inches long and are always cooked before eating. A stroll through any Chinatown will turn up hundreds hanging in butcher shop windows. Once a few slices of pork sausages have been steamed with your rice, or dropped into your stir-fried bok choy, you'll never be happy with those dishes again unless the pork sausage is there.

Coriander. Cilantro and Chinese parsley are two other common names for coriander. Unfortunately, like spinach, garlic, liver, and other distinctively flavored foods, coriander has its share of adamant abstainers. For the rest of us, coriander provides one of the pleasurable flavors of Chinese cooking. If you can't find the fresh herb in your market (don't substitute regular parsley) a small packet of seeds planted in a sunny spot will yield a bountiful supply. Coriander, like regular parsley, may be refrigerated for about a week in a glass of water, covered with a plastic bag. Or, more simply, store it in an inflated, sealable plastic bag containing a tablespoon or so of water.

Chinese Chives. Although regular chives may be substituted, the Chinese variety have a distinct garlic flavor. The 10-inch-long, flat-leafed blades are topped in summer by edible star-shaped white flowers. Chinese chives are sold in small bunches, usually only in oriental markets.

Daikon (Chinese Turnip). The Japanese daikon is a large white variety of radish that can grow to several feet in length. Typically, in United States markets it is usually about a foot long and 3 inches in diameter. It is also known as the Chinese turnip, but is more frequently sold as daikon. The white icicle radish is a possible substitute.

Duck Eggs (Preserved). Also called salted eggs, preserved duck eggs are not to be confused with "thousand-year-old" eggs preserved in lime, which changes the white to a dark wine color and yolks to a dark green. Salted eggs are preserved in a brine solution for about one month, which gives the egg a very salty taste. They are sold packed in dense earth that must be cleaned off. The eggs must be boiled before using.

Egg Roll Skins. Egg roll skins are made from a batter of eggs, flour, salt, and oil. They can be found in supermarkets. Although thicker and less flaky, they are often substituted for the less well distributed spring roll skins. The skins are used as wrappers for many steamed and pan-fried dumplings.

Five-Spice Powder. A strong reddish brown powder that combines ground Szechuan peppercorns, anise, fennel, cloves, and cinnamon.

Ginger Root. Fresh ginger root is a knobby, irregularly shaped root used throughout Asia to flavor food. A knob of the size required is simply broken off, peeled, and either shredded, minced, or squeezed to extract the juice. A garlic press is an excellent tool for this last operation. When purchasing, look for a firm root without soft spots. Ginger root will store well in the vegetable compartment of your refrigerator for two to three weeks.

Hoisin Sauce. Anyone who has enjoyed Peking duck or mu shu pork will immediately know the indispensable rich brown sauce that adds so much to these two dishes. It is a thick, sweet, tangy sauce made from soybeans, sugar, garlic, and spices. It is sold in cans in oriental markets. Once opened, it will keep indefinitely if refrigerated in a covered jar.

Lard. Lard is an age-old cooking fat used all over Asia. It is made by melting down pork fat. The richness of flavor lard imparts to food cooked in it is almost irresistible. The turnip cakes in this book reach their pinnacle of perfection in large part due to the lard used. Lard is also a standard requirement for many deem sum doughs.

Lotus Leaves (Dried). The large round lotus leaf is dried and used as a wrapper to contain a variety of savory foods. The leaves must be thoroughly washed and boiled before using. They are tied together in bunches for sale in oriental markets.

Mustard (Hot). A variety of powdered hot mustards are available on supermarket spice racks. A 2-ounce can of Coleman's is an excellent choice.

Oyster Sauce. A rich, thick, brown Cantonese sauce that is made by cooking oysters in soy sauce and salt water. Although it is sometimes used as a dip, these deem sum recipes use oyster sauce exclusively as a flavoring ingredient in stuffing mixtures. The best variety available here is from the Hop Sing Lung Oyster Sauce Company in Hong Kong. Called "oyster-flavored sauce," it comes in a 14-ounce bottle. It keeps indefinitely when refrigerated.

Plum Sauce. Also known as duck sauce, this is a thick brownish sauce sold in jars or cans in oriental markets. Plums, ginger, chili, vinegar, spices, and sugar combine to give it a lively, spicy, sweet and sour flavor. In this book it is used only as a cooking ingredient, but when diluted with water or fruit preserves, it makes a delicious dip for some of the fried deem sum, such as spring rolls or wonton.

Red Beans. Small Chinese red beans are used to make sweet red bean paste. They are sold in bags by weight in oriental markets.

Red Bean Paste. Chinese red beans are boiled until soft and then puréed in a food processor. Lard is heated in a wok, to which the beans, sugar, and salt are added. The mixture is stirred constantly for about 25 minutes. The result is a dark red paste about the consistency of slightly dry mashed potatoes. It is used in sweet pastries and sweet dishes. Sweet red bean paste is also available in cans in oriental food stores. It will keep for several weeks if stored in covered jars in the refrigerator.

Rice Flour. Short- or long-grain rice is ground to a powder to make rice flour, which is used in deem sum wrapper dough. It is sold in health food and oriental food stores. Stored in a dark place in a tightly covered jar, rice flour will keep indefinitely.

Rice Flour (Glutinous). A powder or flour made from glutinous rice is available in health food stores as well as oriental markets and is used in the preparation of the dough for some deem sum wrappers. Glutinous rice flour will keep indefinitely in a tightly covered jar if stored in a dark area.

Rice (Glutinous). This is a short-grain (almost round) rice often called sweet rice. One of its main characteristics is stickiness, which makes it useful for coating such as in Steamed Pearl Balls (page 38). Glutinous rice needs considerable washing and soaking before use, as described in the recipes.

Saltpeter. Saltpeter, potassium nitrate, has been used historically by the meat-packing industry to increase the reddish color of meat. Chinese chefs also resort to this technique, especially with pork, which would otherwise have an unappetizing gray color. There is a minimum of saltpeter specified in the barbecued pork recipes in this book—just enough to produce a warm reddish brown tone, which we feel makes for richer-looking barbecued meat.

Sesame Oil. A sniff of sesame oil instantly recalls the aroma of the toasted seeds from which this highly flavored oil is derived. It is used primarily as a seasoning, never as a cooking oil. It can be stored perfectly well in a cool, dark cupboard for several months.

Sesame Seeds. Sesame seeds are a common ingredient in oriental cooking. Both black and white seeds are sold. The choice usually depends upon the coloration desired rather than flavor. Sesame seeds are always toasted lightly before using to release their full flavor. Toasting should be done in a dry pan over medium heat for about a minute. Shake and stir the seeds constantly. Remove when the seeds begin to make popping sounds. Grinding, if required, should be done while seeds are hot.

Sesame Seed Paste. Sesame seeds are toasted and then ground to produce a tasty, peanut-butterlike paste.

Shao Hsing Wine. Shao Hsing is a popular Chinese wine that, like Japanese sake, is made from fermented rice. It has a similarly high alcohol content (17.6 percent) and is also often served warm. Similarities end with the taste, however. Shao Hsing tastes like a dry sherry. In fact, a good quality dry sherry substitutes well if Shao Hsing is not available in your area. Like many Western wines, it does double duty as both a cooking and a drinking wine.

Shiu Mye Wrappers. These are round 3-inch skins made from flour and eggs and used for wrapping shiu mye and other deem sum. They are interchangeable with wonton skins except that wonton skins are square. Both are sold in packages of about 100. The choice depends upon the wrapping result desired.

Shrimp (Dried). Tiny shrimp are sun-dried to produce a strongly concentrated salt-flavored condiment that is highly prized in Chinese cooking. Soak before using, as described in the recipes.

Soy Sauce. A salty, brown sauce made by naturally fermenting soybeans, wheat, and salt, soy sauce comes in both light and dark varieties and in a low salt (reduced from 14.8 to 8.8 percent) version. The recipes in this book are made with Kikkoman soy sauce. It is chosen because it is less salty than the popular Chinese brands.

Spring Roll Skins. These are thin skins usually about 6 inches square used for wrapping spring rolls. They are made from flour and water and are very fragile and flaky when fried. A heavier egg roll skin may be substituted, but it will not have the same delicacy. It is best to purchase commercially available spring roll skins. They are available in oriental markets.

Szechuan Pepper. Szechuan peppercorns are toasted and then ground in a blender to produce a hot seasoning powder.

Tapioca Starch. A white, flourlike substance, this is often combined with wheat starch in making deem sum wrappers because of the crisp texture it produces.

Taro Root. The starchy tuberous root of the tropical taro plant, taro root comes in many shapes and sizes, but the kind you will probably find will be about the size of a small grapefruit with a dirty brown skin. The skin is peeled and the white, fibrous, potatolike interior is always cooked before eating.

Water Chestnuts. The water chestnut is a small, brown-skinned, chestnut-shaped root, which must be peeled to reach the sweet, crunchy interior meat. Water chestnuts are grown in the United States and are occasionally available fresh in supermarkets. An alternative is the canned version, but it falls far short of the flavor and crunchiness of the fresh product. Jicama is also an excellent substitute.

Water Chestnut Powder. Ground water chestnuts produce a powder that is used for extra crispiness in deep-fried foods or pastries.

Wheat Starch. The residue of wheat flour after protein removal, it is sold by the pound in Chinese grocery stores. Store it as you would flour.

Wonton Skins. These are thin 3-inch-square wrappings for wonton made from flour and eggs and interchangeable with shiu mye skins except that shiu mye skins are round. They are inexpensive and sold in packages of 100.

Chicken Crescents p. 20

Beef Baskets p. 22

Four Color Dumplings p. 24

Shrimp Moons p. 26

Barbecued Pork Buns   p. 28

Beef and Watercress   p. 30

Steamed Spareribs   p. 32

Mandarin Dumplings   p. 34

Rice Noodle Rolls   p. 36

Steamed Pearl Balls   p. 38

Lotus Leaf Rice   p. 40

Shrimp Goldfish   p. 44

Shrimp Toast   p. 48

Chicken Lollipops   p. 50

Spring Rolls   p. 52

Taro Dumplings   p. 56

Sweet Rice Dumplings   p. 58

Bean Curd Skin Rolls   p. 60

Fried Fish Balls   p. 64

Silver-Wrapped Chicken   p. 66

Cream Cheese Wonton   p. 68

Stuffed Crab Claws   p. 70

Pot Stickers   p. 74

Turnip Cakes   p. 76

Stuffed Bean Curd   p. 78

Barbecued Pork   p. 82

Golden Coin Pork   p. 84

Barbecued Spareribs   p. 86

Chicken Turnovers p. 88

Custard Tarts p. 92

Sesame Seed Balls p. 94

Black Sesame Rolls p. 96

TECHNIQUES AND TOOLS

STIR-FRYING

If you like action-packed sizzle, then stir-fry cooking is the best show in the Yank Sing kitchen. Unlike the unobtrusive steamer that quietly does its thing, the stir-fry technique lets everyone know something important is happening. Oil and food hiss at each other, steel spatulas clatter and clang, geysers of steam erupt at the drop of a bok choy—and in minutes the delicious result is ladled onto a warm serving plate and sent off to a table of hungry diners. Next order, please.

The heart of the stir-fry technique is the well-seasoned, round-bottomed steel wok. The wok seems to have been made for stir-frying. Its rounded exterior smoothly draws the flame up, evenly heating the sides. The concave interior basin is ideal for all of the tossing, mixing, and pushing to and fro that stir-frying requires to properly sear the foods, blend in the seasonings and sauces, and generally keep things moving. The flat-bottomed wok is a good second choice for those of you with gas equipment, and essential if you are cooking on electric burners. Your technique will fall a little short of the smooth performance possible with the former, but results will still be excellent. The flat-bottomed wok is still a reassuringly deep, wide receptacle that helps keep your food in the pan during this sort of active cooking. If it has been well seasoned over the course of a dozen or so meals, it, like its round-bottomed cousin, will be a joy to use. If your kitchen is wokless, and you don't want to invest just yet, get out your largest steel skillet. The results will be just fine.

The only remaining tools of the stir-fry trade are the wide, long-handled steel spatula, the steel ladle, and the wok cover that traps moisture to steam-fry foods to completion. The spatula keeps everything tossing and turning. The ladle scoops things out, or pours things in. And together they can perform some mighty lifting jobs. Neither tool is dainty. They are sturdy, large, and well suited to the job.

The key to successful stir-frying is not in the process itself,

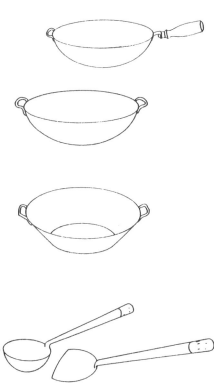

but in the preparation. Since the idea is to cook foods rapidly, sealing in their flavorful juices, you must have everything ready, and a clear idea of the order in which the ingredients will be cooked. Often, the chopping and organizing can be done a day ahead and the foods refrigerated until needed.

Once things are in order, preheat the wok over high heat for about a minute. When a bead of water dropped on the steel sizzles and immediately evaporates, it is ready for the oil. Pour a ring of oil (about 2 or 3 tablespoons) around the wok about halfway up the sides and allow it to drain toward the bottom, coating as it goes. Complete the coating job by spreading the oil with the spatula to eliminate dry spots.

Give the oil a few moments to heat up, and then stir-fry a small sample of the food you will be cooking. The oil should be sizzling hot, sealing in luscious juices without burning. Adjust your heat and then add the oil flavorings (garlic, ginger, etc.) given in the recipes. Stir them for half a minute or so to flavor the oil thoroughly. Leave the flavorings in the oil, and add the ingredients in the order specified by the recipes. Vigorous stir-frying is important now, to prevent burning and to insure that foods are seared on all sides. Things are to be cooked to the "just done" stage. Extra oil should be on hand in case the wok becomes too dry and the food begins sticking. If so, push the food to one side with the spatula and run a little oil down the cleared side of the wok to prewarm it before allowing it to contact the food.

Uniform chopping and shredding will insure that things cook to completion in the same amount of time. Slower cooking hard vegetables (carrots, broccoli, lotus root, and the like) will require more time, so put them in a few moments before the faster cooking vegetables such as sprouts or bok choy. Occasionally, a recipe will require that liquids be added and the wok covered to complete the cooking in steam.

STEAMING

If you are equipped with a good wok and a sturdy set of steamer trays you have all you need in the way of "hardware" to perform most of the wonders of deem sum cooking. A few additional utensils, such as a vegetable cleaver and a mesh strainer, and you are on your way. The wok tackles the stir- and deep-frying, while the steamer produces the gentle, moist heat that delivers up those tender steamed delights. A nice balance.

If one were to rate cooking methods on the basis of simplicity and economy against final results, the grand prize would have to be given to the steaming process. It cooks while retaining all of the moisture, flavor, nutrition, and aroma of the ingredients by the simplest of all procedures—boiling water in a container. The steamer itself can be improvised. It simply requires a large, covered pot, partly filled with boiling water, and a method of suspending the food in the resulting steam. But if improvisation is not an economic necessity, then, by all means, invest in a good steamer. You will be amply repaid.

The Steamer. An early dividend is the discovery that the steamer, like an urban skyscraper, economizes on space by building upward rather than outward. Steamer trays can be stacked three or four high over a single pot of boiling water, each layer cooking independently and unattended until the timer bell rings. This is no trifle as any busy cook with a crowded stovetop knows. For that matter, the steamer may be removed from the cooking area entirely if a portable hotplate is available.

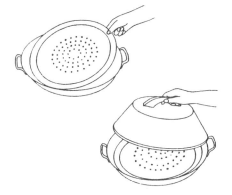

The simplest wok-type steaming arrangement can be assembled with a round perforated tray that seats itself in the wok. When used with the wok cover this arrangement provides a roomy, single-tier steaming compartment. Other wok inserts, such as wooden or metal crossbars, are also available in stores that carry oriental products. Likewise, a variety of collapsible and noncollapsible stands can be purchased. They are set directly in the boiling water, with the plate of food perched on top. All are handy for quickly assembling a simple steaming unit, when multiple steamer trays are not called for.

The metal steamer. This steamer is excellent if all-around efficiency, easy cleaning, and durability are desired. To begin with, the metal steamer comes with its own water container, which makes it unnecessary to devote a useful wok to the mundane chore of boiling water. The steamer is a self-contained unit with water container (base), two steamer compartments, and lid, all of which fit neatly together. There is a very nice Japanese stainless steel steamer on the market that is square with rounded corners. The square shape offers

slightly more space than a round steamer of a given diameter and so may be more useful to you.

If there is any disadvantage to the metal steamer, it is that it tends to produce a considerable amount of interior condensation, which can find its way onto the food. The domelike steamer lid and interior construction are designed to drain water off to the sides and are generally effective. If condensation is a major problem, or if you are working with a flat lid, a dish towel placed beneath the lid with its corners pulled up outside and tied on top will trap all of the moisture. One other consideration with the metal steamer is that the metal becomes quite hot, much hotter than bamboo. For this reason, chefs will usually line the steamer trays with dampened cheesecloth, or use plates, rather than place food directly on the hot metal.

The bamboo steamer. Bamboo is one of the fastest-growing plants in the world, generally reaching its full towering height in two months. It can grow half the height of a man in a single day. It is also the single most useful plant to half of the human race because it can be used to make everything from homes and bridges to the smallest culinary utensil—the toothpick. It is as if nature wanted to give man an adaptable raw material equal to his ingenuity. We have to confess a fondness for the traditional bamboo steamer. It is used throughout this book. For the water container we use a flat-bottomed wok reserved primarily for this purpose. We do not recommend this arrangement as ideal. It simply is comfortable for us, and our old, well-used steamer imparts a delicate bamboo flavor to the food that we have come to fancy.

Bamboo steamers have two great attributes. Most water condensation is absorbed into the fiber, so this ceases to be a problem. And the material makes an excellent insulator, so very little heat is lost. This is increasingly important as more trays are added to the stack. On this point, three to four trays are possible, but ambitious. This many trays will require a strong heat source, and some checking to insure that top and bottom trays are heating equally. Some tray juggling midway through the steaming process may be necessary to even out the cooking times. A nice benefit of the bamboo steamer is that it may be used as an attractive serving tray, carried directly to the table from the stove. For deem sum, small four-inch steamers are available, which make delightful individual servers.

When picking out a bamboo steamer, be sure that it looks sturdy and uses no metal (which will rust) in its manufacture. Its different pieces should fit snugly together without wobbling or sticking. It is good practice to soak the dry steamer in water for about fifteen minutes before each use. Clean it thoroughly when finished. A very diluted mild detergent and scrub brush will do the job effectively. The steamer should be air dried, and, if it will not be used for some time, it may be stored in a large plastic bag and tied securely. With such care, your steamer will last for many years.

Steaming Procedure. The first step in the steaming procedure has been mentioned: Soak the bamboo baskets for about fifteen minutes. Towel-dry the baskets, and if food is to be placed directly on the trays, they should be oiled.

Place enough water in the wok to reach within one inch of the lower steamer basket. Some chefs will put in enough water to slightly submerge the lower rim, which they feel protects the steamer against excessive heat from the wok. What is important is that the boiling water not splash up onto the food. You want to strike a balance, using enough water so the wok does not boil dry, but not so much that the food gets wet. Most deem sum dumplings will be cooked in less than fifteen minutes, so it may not be necessary to replenish the water during cooking, but it is good practice to have a supply of boiling water standing by for this purpose.

Bring the water to a full boil, and let the steamer fill with steam to preheat it thoroughly. The steamer trays can then be removed, filled with food, and reassembled over the steam. If you are careful, food can be added directly to the steamer as it is steaming, but it is usually safer to remove the tray and return it. (Steam can give you a bad burn.) In all cases, when opening a steamer, tilt open the far end first so the steam exhausts away from you. Allow the steam to disperse before doing anything. If food is to be steamed on a plate (to gather its juices) the plate should be at least one to two inches smaller in diameter than the steamer to permit free circulation. Always arrange dumplings with space in between each to allow for circulation and to prevent them from sticking together. The final bit of advice is—don't peek. The recommended times will produce good results. What is an inviolate rule in oven cooking is equally binding in steaming. Unfortunately, no one has put a glass window in a steamer yet.

DEEP-FRYING

A nagging uneasiness settles on the soul when the time comes to deal with a large pot of very hot oil. It usually intensifies in relation to the size of the object you are cooking. Fortunately, with deem sum the emphasis is on bite-size delights so the larger deep-fry challenges can be left for another time.

Usually, restaurants produce the best deep-fried foods. The professional chef develops a feeling for the oil by working with it daily. Most have an infallible sense of its temperature and an uncanny ability to pluck the morsel out at the moment of perfect doneness. Also, volume business allows the restaurant chef to establish proper procedures for using, storing, and discarding the oil. At Yank Sing, specially designed, thermostatically controlled deep-frying units permit perfect control at all times. Naturally, the home cook who deep-fries only occasionally cannot match this expertise. But with proper home technique great results are possible.

Two physical factors are basic to deep-fat frying. First, oil can be heated roughly two to three times as hot as water, and second, oil and water don't mix. What this means is that very hot oil can be used to quickly create a crispy exterior shell sealing a food and permitting it to cook in its own flavorful juices. If the oil is at the proper temperature, the steamy moisture of the food will repel it upon contact to produce a crispy, oil-free, delicious deem sum.

The first consideration is the oil itself. For our purposes, a flavor-free blended vegetable oil is an excellent choice. Peanut oil is a universal favorite for Chinese style deep-frying but it is more expensive. It is somewhat heavier and imparts a mild nutty flavor to the food.

There is no common agreement on when to discard the oil. The simplest and best guideline is that its time has come when you don't like the way the food is coming out! Generally speaking, the oil will show its age by darkening considerably. Older oil will produce darker food, so avoid it if a light golden crust is desired. Light or delicate-tasting items such as shrimp balls should always be cooked in fresh oil.

Unlike people, oil doesn't forget as it ages. Memories of flavors past accumulate with each use and are unselfishly
shared with all newcomers. Sometimes unwanted flavors can
be eliminated by cooking a few slices of peeled potato or ginger root in oil at 375°F. until they are golden (remove and
discard). Always strain used oil thoroughly when returning it to
its container. Stir it briefly while hot to dispel any trapped
moisture. Skim any debris from the surface. Allow it to cool to
room temperature. A large glass jar with a screw top makes a
good storage container, since it permits you to inspect the oil
visually for color. The jar should have a wide mouth capable
of accepting a wire mesh strainer directly. It is helpful if the
strainer sits atop the jar unassisted so that both hands can be
devoted to the pouring operation. The strainer should be lined
with several layers of cheesecloth and the oil poured through.
It should be stored in a cool, dark place. Oil that has been
used to cook fish will often retain a strong fishy odor so you
might consider storing it separately for fish use only. Labeling
the oil is a good idea, to remind you how often it has been
used and for what.

Before leaving our discussion of oil, a few words about
safety are in order. The first precaution is: Never leave oil unattended on the burner. The second is to have a cover, such
as a wok cover, nearby during the entire cooking operation.
Quickly covering a flaming wok effectively squelches the
flames. An oil-type fire extinguisher is also vital should the
flame begin to spread. Never, ever try to douse an oil fire with
water. Constantly be alert to signs of smoke coming from the
oil. This is a signal that it is approaching its flaming point.

Another characteristic of hot oil, while not as devastating as
its fire potential, is its propensity to spit and pop when in contact with water. The reaction is unavoidable, but you can
minimize it by making sure to pat all foods thoroughly dry before introducing them to the oil. Long sleeves are good
protection from spitting oil. A very helpful circular metal
screen is manufactured, which can be held like a shield to
fend off attacking missiles. Another helpful device is the Chinese mesh strainer with a long bamboo handle, which is used
to lower the food into the oil. It permits good distance between you and the erupting oil. Extra long Chinese cooking
chopsticks are also used for long-distance handling, but are
only helpful if one is adept with chopsticks.

The wok, of course, has become well known in America in

the last decade or so. Cooking stores routinely sell them in a variety of styles (even electric woks!) right along with other pots and pans. It is generally recognized that the wok's effectiveness in deep-frying rests with the fact that its spherical shape presents the largest surface area (where the frying takes place) of oil to volume. In other words, you can deep-fry with about one-third less oil than you would need in a conventional pot. It has been argued with some merit that "the more oil the better" in deep-frying since a large amount of oil can hold heat better and is less subject to temperature fluctuations. But for the home cook, who cannot handle large quantities of hot oil easily, the wok is a great convenience, and Chinese chefs have managed very well indeed with their one-third less oil.

The round-bottomed wok is superior in stir-frying, but for deep-frying in the home kitchen, the flat-bottomed wok with its extra stability is probably the best choice. Round-bottomed woks are mated to conventional Western stovetops by the use of a wok ring. This is a totally unworkable arrangement with an electric range, and only partially successful with gas. It raises the wok too far from the heat source and only barely solves the stability problem, which is of serious concern with deep hot oil.

Gas is preferable to electric heat for deep-frying because quick, precise adjustments of the heat source are essential if the oil is to be maintained at a constant temperature. The usual solution with sluggish electric ranges is to transfer the cooking vessel to another burner of different temperature, or off the coils entirely to change heat quickly. This is not easily or safely done with a big container of hot oil, although the wok makes this operation a bit more manageable. Thermostatically controlled woks, or Western style deep-fryers, if they have proven accurate and dependable, are good solutions in an electric kitchen.

For the home cook who does a great deal of Chinese cooking, a built-in stainless steel 20,000 BTU wok burner installation is manufactured for the home kitchen by the Robert Yick Company, 261 Bayshore Boulevard, San Francisco, CA 94124; (415) 282-9707. It drops directly into a tiled countertop and comes with a stainless steel lid that folds down level with the counter to cover the entire unit when not in use. The unit is made of heavy gauge stainless steel to commercial standards and is a joy to use for Chinese and non-Chinese cooking alike.

To begin deep-frying, the wok itself should first be warmed briefly. Then pour in four to six cups of oil and heat over moderate heat to slightly more than the temperature required by the recipe. This will compensate for the cooling effect of the food when first inserted.

For the occasional deep-fry cook temperature control is best determined with a thermometer. The dial type that can be clamped to the side of the wok is the best choice. Chinese chefs who prefer less instrumentation will simply insert a dry chopstick deep into the oil and judge the temperature by the quantity of frothy bubbles rising from the wood. Another method is to drop a bit of the food or batter to be fried into the oil and watch its reaction. If it rises, sizzling, to the surface in a few seconds, the oil is at about 375°F., which is suitable for most deem sum frying. This temperature will produce a golden, crisp, oil-free exterior crust and a moist, well-cooked interior. If the test sample doesn't sink at all, but does a frothy sizzling dance around the top of the oil, the temperature is well into the 400° range and will be much too hot for tiny deem sum. The exteriors will burn before the interiors have a chance to cook. Such high temperatures are only satisfactory for larger fish or fowl whose size and greater moisture content can withstand a higher heat. If the test morsel sinks to the bottom with only mild bubbling, the temperature is too low for deem sum—probably in the 250° to 275° range—and will produce an oily pastry. But most home cooks will probably do better to leave these testing methods to the experts, and depend instead on the thermometer, still the most reliable way to keep oil at recommended temperatures. Needless to say, the best test of the food is the one chefs have always used. Namely, cook one or two deem sum and sample them!

The oil cooking process itself is straightforward. Because deem sum are small they are easily immersed in the oil with usually only mild spattering, so fingers are a "handy" tool, but *only* for putting the tidbits in—never for removing them. The Chinese also make a wire mesh strainer in different sizes; this can be used for both inserting and retrieving food. A six- or eight-inch version is good for deem sum. The coarsely woven strainer is attached to a twelve- to fourteen-inch bamboo handle. The strainer should be warmed in the oil first, to prevent food from sticking to it. Once you use it for deep-frying, we are sure you will come to favor it over all other strainers. It is a lightweight, handsomely crafted tool that cradles the food securely. Long oriental cooking chopsticks are another useful tool for those of you who are handy with chopsticks. Food can be inserted, turned, or plucked out of the oil with the flick of a chopstick. Long wooden or metal tongs are another good choice.

Food should be at room temperature and as dry as possible. Generally, only a few pastries should be fried at a time. As one becomes done, remove it and add another. Working your way through in this manner minimizes the temperature fluctuations of the oil and allows you to keep an eye on things. Most pastries will be done in about three to four minutes. They should be turned once or twice during this time to insure even cooking and browning. Extra crispy results can be achieved by double-frying—removing the partially cooked pastry to drain and cool, then refrying it to completion before serving. When done, remove and drain on absorbent paper toweling or a wire rack.

Fried foods should be served promptly. This is the rationale behind the Japanese tempura bar, which allows service direct from chef to customer. At Yank Sing only a few deem sum carts are filled at a time and quickly rolled to the customers. Deem sum is at its best at crowded times when the food carts roll continually and nothing lasts long. Unlike Western restaurants, the best seats are right outside the kitchen door, from which vantage point the choicest, hottest pastries can be snatched.

STEAMED DISHES

CHICKEN CRESCENTS

Gai nup fun gwor

Chicken is the main filling ingredient for these delicious deem sum. Smaller amounts of mushrooms, bamboo shoots, scallion, pork, and shrimp complete the mixture. A thin har gow dough, which permits a tempting peek at the ingredients through the translucent skin, is used for the wrappers.

1. Soak dried mushrooms in tepid water to cover for about 30 minutes, or until soft and pliable. When reconstituted, cut off and discard stems, and mince caps.

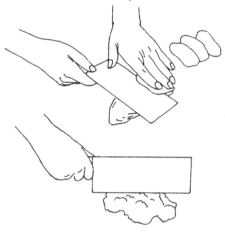

2. Slice chicken breast against the grain at an angle, and coarsely mince.

3. Combine all filling ingredients.

4. Mix seasoning ingredients together and reserve.

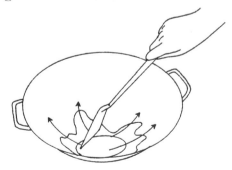

5. Heat 2 tablespoons oil in wok at high heat. With the steel spatula, coat the sides of the wok with hot oil.

6. Add filling and stir-fry over high heat until chicken and pork turn white. Stir in reserved seasoning and stir-fry for another minute. Remove from heat. Cool to handling temperature.

7. Prepare har gow wrappers. Press out 3-inch-diameter disks with oiled tortilla press.

8. Soak bamboo steamer in water for about 15 minutes.

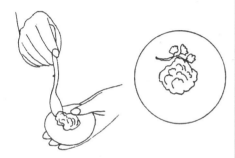

9. Take a leaf of coriander and lay it on one side of har gow wrapper.

10. Add 1 heaping teaspoon of filling.

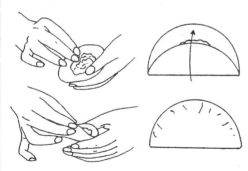

11. Fold other side of wrapper over and pinch edges to seal. Repeat with remaining wrappers and filling.

12. Place crescents on an oiled plate, cover with plastic wrap, and refrigerate until ready to steam.

13. Wipe steamer dry, and lightly oil inside steamer bottom. Place hot water in wok to come within 1 inch of the bottom of steamer. Have additional hot water on hand to replenish as necessary.

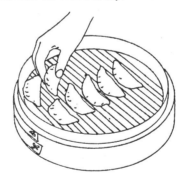

14. Arrange crescents in steamer, leaving space between each. Cover, set steamer in wok over rapidly boiling water, and steam for 15 minutes.

15. Allow the dumplings to cool for a minute or two before removing them from the steamer. Har gow dough tends to tear when very hot.

16. Serve with Soy Sauce–Chili Pepper Oil–Vinegar Dip (page 114)

To make about 30

Filling:
6 dried black Chinese mushrooms
8 ounces chicken breast, boned and skinned
3 ounces bamboo shoots, finely shredded
2 inches scallion, white part only, minced
2 ounces bay shrimp, minced
4 ounces ground pork, with medium fat

Seasoning:
½ teaspoon salt
2 teaspoons sugar
1 teaspoon soy sauce
¼ teaspoon ground white pepper
1 teaspoon sesame oil
1 tablespoon Shao Hsing wine or dry sherry
2 teaspoons tapioca starch

2 tablespoons vegetable oil

30 Har Gow Dough wrappers (page 100)
Oil
30 coriander leaves
Soy Sauce–Chili Pepper Oil–Vinegar Dip (page 114)

BEEF BASKETS

Gnow yuk shiu mye

In this recipe, the shiu mye wrappers are formed into a basket shape by pleating completely around. Sometimes a pea or other tidbit garnishes the open top. Shiu mye wrappers are available in almost all oriental markets. Wonton wrappers are interchangeable with them but must be trimmed to a circle shape first.

1. Mince coriander, scallion, ginger, and lemon peel. (Use a vegetable peeler for peeling the lemon so that just the zest is removed.)

2. Combine filling ingredients in a bowl. Mix thoroughly with a wooden spatula or chopsticks until smooth and tacky. Refrigerate for 1 hour.

3. Soak bamboo steamer in water for about 15 minutes.

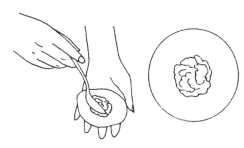

4. Place a heaping teaspoon of filling on a shiu mye wrapper.

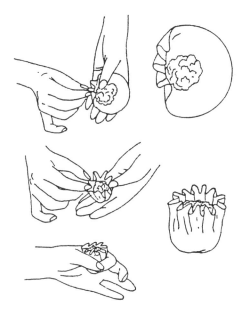

5. Hold in one hand, as shown, and begin pleating around, pressing the skin into the filling to hold. The more pleats the better.

6. Make remaining dumplings. If preparing ahead, place on an oiled plate, cover with plastic wrap, and refrigerate or freeze until ready to steam.

7. Wipe steamer dry and lightly oil inside steamer bottom.

8. Place hot water in wok to come within 1 inch of the bottom of steamer. Have additional hot water on hand to replenish as necessary.

9. Arrange dumplings on steamer rack, leaving space between each. Cover and steam over rapidly boiling water for 10 minutes.

10. Serve with Soy Sauce–Chili Pepper Oil Dip.

To make about 20

Filling:
2 tablespoons minced
   coriander
1 tablespoon minced
   scallion, equal parts
   white and green
½ teaspoon minced
   ginger root
¼ teaspoon minced
   lemon peel
8 ounces ground chuck
¼ teaspoon salt
¼ teaspoon sugar
1 teaspoon soy sauce
¼ teaspoon ground
   white pepper
½ teaspoon sesame oil
2 teaspoons oyster
   sauce
¼ cup Chicken Stock
   (page 116)
1 tablespoon Shao
   Hsing wine or dry
   sherry
1 tablespoon tapioca
   starch

20 shiu mye or wonton
   wrappers
Oil

Soy Sauce–Chili Pepper
   Oil Dip (page 114)

23

FOUR COLOR DUMPLINGS

Say sik shiu mye

These deem sum delicacies are named after the distinctive way the shiu mye wrapper is folded. Four pockets are formed to contain a garnish of a pea, mushroom, shrimp, and carrot. The filling is a tasty pork-mushroom combination.

1. Dice carrot into 30 pea-size pieces. Blanch until just tender. Reserve for garnish. Shell and measure peas. Prepare shrimp. Dice shrimp into 30 pea-size pieces. Mince remaining shrimp for filling.

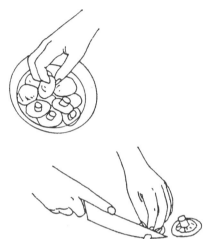

2. Soak all 12 dried mushrooms in tepid water to cover for about 30 minutes, or until soft and pliable. When reconstituted, cut off stems and discard. Dice 3 caps into 30 pea-size pieces and reserve for garnish. Mince remaining caps for filling. You now have approximately 30 pieces each of carrots, peas, shrimp, and black mushrooms for garnish.

3. Combine 9 minced black mushrooms with remaining filling ingredients in bowl. Mix thoroughly with a wooden spatula or chopsticks until smooth and tacky.

4. Soak bamboo steamer in water for about 15 minutes.

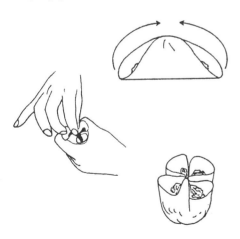

5. Spoon about 1 tablespoon of filling onto a wrapper.

6. Moisten the edge of the wrapper with water, fold in half, and tightly pinch the center, as shown.

7. Make a quarter turn, bring the edges to the center, and tightly pinch again. This makes four pockets, as shown.

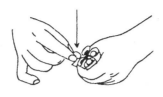

8. Garnish each pocket with a piece of mushroom, shrimp, carrot, and pea.

9. Make remaining dumplings. If preparing ahead, place on oiled plate and cover with plastic wrap. Refrigerate or freeze until ready to steam.

10. Wipe steamer basket dry and lightly oil inside steamer bottom.

11. Place hot water in wok to reach 1 inch from the steamer bottom. Have additional hot water available to replenish as necessary.

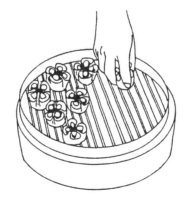

12. Arrange dumplings in steamer, leaving space between each. Cover and steam over rapidly boiling water for 15 minutes.

13. Serve with Mustard Soy Sauce Dip.

To make about 30

Garnishes:
3 dried black
  mushrooms
1 small carrot
30 fresh shelled peas
2 ounces shrimp,
  shelled, deveined, and
  cleaned

Filling:
9 small dried Chinese
  black mushrooms
2 tablespoons minced
  scallion, equal parts
  white and green
4 large fresh button
  mushrooms, coarsely
  minced
8 ounces ground pork
  with medium fat
¾ teaspoon salt
1 teaspoon sugar
1 tablespoon soy sauce
1 tablespoon oyster
  sauce
2 teaspoons sesame oil
2 tablespoons Shao
  Hsing wine or dry
  sherry
2 tablespoons tapioca
  starch

Oil
24 shiu mye wrappers

Mustard Soy Sauce Dip
  (page 115)

SHRIMP MOONS

Har gow

This irresistible little half-moon-shaped shrimp dumpling is one of the classics of deem sum cookery. The white har gow wrapper is made from wheat starch, which becomes translucent when steamed, displaying its succulent filling. The bamboo steamer imparts a slight bamboo flavor to the delicate shrimp mixture—a thoroughly pleasing combination.

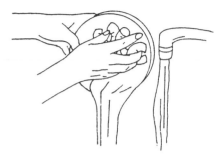

1. Shell and devein shrimp. Place in a bowl, sprinkle with 1 teaspoon of salt and mix well with the fingers. Rinse in several changes of cold water and drain thoroughly.

2. Dice shrimp to large pea size. You want the springy quality of the shrimp, not the mushiness that would result from mincing.

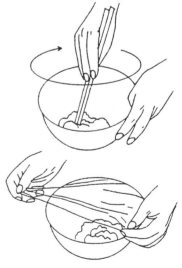

3. Place shrimp, pork fat, and bamboo shoots in a bowl and add ½ teaspoon salt. Add sugar, pepper, tapioca starch, and wine. Mix thoroughly, cover, and refrigerate for 2 hours.

4. Prepare Har Gow Dough wrappers. Press out 3-inch-diameter disks with oiled tortilla press.

5. Soak bamboo steamer in water for about 10 minutes.

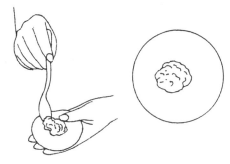

6. Place about a teaspoon of filling mixture on a har gow wrapper.

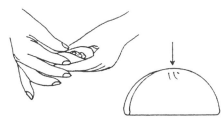

7. Fold in half (making a half-moon shape) and pinch at the center.

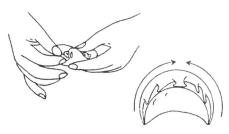

8. Pleat and press edges together to seal. Work from each end toward center. Form dumpling into half-moon shape as you pleat.

9. Prepare all of the dumplings in this manner. Place on an oiled plate, cover with plastic wrap, and refrigerate or freeze until ready to steam.

10. Wipe steamer basket dry and lightly oil the inside bottom.

11. Place hot water in wok to come within 1 inch of the bottom of the steamer. Boil over high heat. Have additional hot water on hand to replenish as necessary.

12. Arrange dumplings in steamer, leaving space between each. Cover and steam over rapidly boiling water for 10 minutes.

13. Serve with Soy Sauce–Chili Pepper Oil–Vinegar Dip.

To make about 30

Filling:
8 ounces shrimp
1½ teaspoons salt
1½ ounces pork fat, minced fine
½ cup finely shredded bamboo shoots
½ teaspoon sugar
⅛ teaspoon ground white pepper
1 tablespoon tapioca starch
1 tablespoon Shao Hsing wine or dry sherry

30 Har Gow Dough wrappers (see page 100)
Vegetable oil

Soy Sauce–Chili Pepper Oil–Vinegar Dip (page 114)

BARBECUED PORK BUNS

Char shiu bow

The pork bun is a light, slightly sweet, fluffy bun with a filling of diced barbecued pork in its own distinctive sauce. No Westerner can take his first stroll through Chinatown without wondering about the curious white pork buns stacked one atop the other in restaurant windows. The adventurous soon try them and discover one of China's great luncheon treats.

1. Prepare Basic Bun Dough.

2. Combine sauce ingredients in small bowl and reserve.

3. Prepare filling ingredients, keeping them separate.

4. Heat 3 tablespoons of oil in wok at high heat. Using the steel spatula, coat the sides of the wok about half-way up with hot oil.

5. Add diced onion and stir-fry until transparent.

6. Add diced barbecued pork and stir-fry for about 2 minutes.

7. Stir sauce and add to the mixture. Stir-fry until it thickens. Set aside to cool to room temperature, and refrigerate. (It is easier to handle when cold.)

8. Soak bamboo steamer in water for about 10 minutes. Dry and lightly oil each compartment bottom.

9. Punch the dough down and divide in half.

10. Reserve one of the halves under a damp towel. Roll the other half into a cylinder about 1½ inches in diameter.

11. Cut into 12 equal portions and cover with damp towel.

12. Flatten one of the pieces between palms.

13. With a small rolling pin, roll the disk out to 4 inches in diameter. Roll the edge thinner than the center.

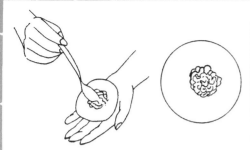

14. Place a tablespoon of filling at the center.

15. Begin pleating the edges of the dough, forming a pocket for the filling.

16. Gently guide the filling into the pocket with the left thumb.

17. Continue pleating around to complete the pocket while guiding the filling into it with the thumb.

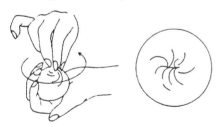

18. Close off the top by twisting the pleats together.

19. Attach a wax paper square to the sealed end and place, paper side down, in oiled steamer basket. (If you don't have enough baskets to hold 24 buns, then place the extras on an oiled baking pan or cookie

sheet until time to steam. Cover with a floured towel.)

20. Continue the rolling and filling procedures until you have made the first 12 buns. Repeat with remaining ingredients.

21. Allow at least 2 inches between buns. Set in a warm place, still covered with a floured towel, and let rise for 45 minutes to 1 hour.

22. Place hot water in wok to come within 1 inch of the bottom of steamer. Boil water over high heat. Have additional hot water on hand to replenish as necessary.

23. Arrange pork buns on steamer rack, leaving space between each. Cover, set steamer in wok over rapidly boiling hot water, and steam for 10 minutes. Do not remove the lid while steaming. It will stop dough from rising.

24. Pork buns may also be baked; preheat your oven to 350°F.

25. Beat 1 egg with 1 tablespoon of water.

26. Place the buns, well separated, on a baking sheet and brush each with egg.

27. Bake for 20 minutes or until golden brown.

28. Remove and brush on melted sweet butter or lard.

29. Serve the buns with Soy Sauce–Chili Pepper Oil Dip.

30. Both steamed and baked Barbecued Pork Buns freeze beautifully, so make extras. To reheat frozen steamed buns, steam for 20 to 30 minutes. Wrap frozen baked buns in foil and heat for 30 minutes in a preheated 250°F. oven.

To make 24
1 recipe Basic Bun
    Dough (page 104)

Sauce ingredients:
1 tablespoon hoisin
    sauce
1 tablespoon catsup
2 tablespoons oyster
    sauce
2 tablespoons soy
    sauce
¼ cup packed brown
    sugar
¼ teaspoon white
    pepper
2 tablespoons
    cornstarch
½ cup Chicken Stock
    (page 116)
1 tablespoon Shao
    Hsing wine or dry
    sherry

Filling:
1 medium-sized onion,
    diced pea size
10 ounces Barbecued
    Pork (see page 82)
    diced pea size

3 tablespoons oil
Additional oil for
    steamer
24 two-inch-square
    pieces wax paper

For baking:
1 egg beaten with 1
    tablespoon water
4 tablespoons sweet
    butter or lard, melted

Soy Sauce–Chili Pepper
    Oil Dip (page 114)

BEEF AND WATERCRESS

Sai choy ngow yuk

In earlier steamer recipes, dumplings have been placed directly on the reeds of the steamer with the intention that any condensation be drained off to prevent sogginess. We have included this recipe to introduce you to the ambrosial juices that can be produced and collected in the steaming process. The beef balls are meant to be served well saturated with the flavorsome liquid and tender watercress combination.

1. Rinse watercress under cold running water. Drain. Pinch off the tough stems and dscard.

2. Spread the watercress out on a heatproof (Pyrex) dish.

3. Combine beef mixture in a bowl and mix well until tacky. Thorough mixing will eliminate air pockets that can cause the meat to break apart during steaming.

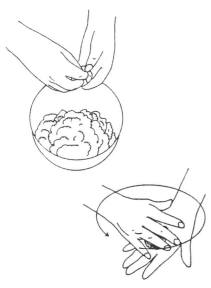

4. Wet hands with water and take up a heaping teaspoon of mixture. Roll between palms to form a ball. Set aside. Repeat with remaining mixture.

5. Dust each ball lightly with cornstarch and place on the watercress bed in a single layer.

6. Fill wok with water to 1 inch below the round perforated tray.

7. Cover with wok cover and bring water to rapid boil.

8. Place the beef ball plate on the perforated tray, cover, and steam for 15 minutes.

9. Remove from steamer.

10. Serve hot in preheated bowl. Pour collected liquid and watercress over the beef balls.

To make 24 balls
1 bunch watercress
(about 6 ounces)

Beef mixture:
1 pound coarsely
ground chuck
½ cup minced scallion
1 teaspoon minced
ginger root
12 water chestnuts,
minced
1 teaspoon sugar
1¼ teaspoons salt
1 teaspoon soy sauce
1½ tablespoons oyster
sauce
1 tablespoon Shao
Hsing wine or dry
sherry
1 egg, beaten
1 teaspoon sesame oil
⅛ teaspoon ground
white pepper
1 tablespoon tapioca
starch

Cornstarch for dusting

STEAMED SPARERIBS

See jup pai gwut

Like Beef and Watercress (page 30), this is another example of the superlative flavors possible when food is allowed to steam in its own collected juices. In this case, for added flavor, the bite-size backribs are steamed while still immersed in the marinade. Don't forget to ask your butcher to cut the ribs into bite-size pieces for you. It is a difficult operation for the home kitchen.

1. Put spareribs in large bowl and place under running water for 10 to 15 minutes to remove blood from bone and plump the meat. Drain and set aside.

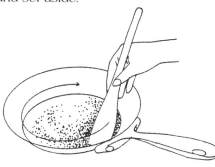

2. Dry-toast about ¼ cup of Szechuan peppercorns in a small frying pan over low heat until fragrant. Stir continuously to prevent browning. Store this supply in a covered jar for future use. Using a small coffee grinder or blender, grind about ½ teaspoon for this recipe.

3. Combine ground Szechuan peppercorns, sugar, soy sauce, oyster sauce, wine, orange juice, and sesame oil in a bowl.

4. Slice chili pepper into rounds, retaining seeds.

5. Break off a small piece of ginger root. Peel, and mash beneath flat side of cleaver. Mince and add.

6. Repeat with enough garlic cloves to yield 1 tablespoon minced garlic.

7. Place salted black beans in cup and cover with cold water. Mix with fingers and drain. Repeat twice more.

8. Mash rinsed black beans with side of cleaver. Mince. Add to marinade.

9. Mince scallion whites. Add. Mix marinade well.

10. Pat spareribs dry and place in deep heatproof dish to fit your steamer. Sprinkle tapioca starch over ribs and mix by hand to coat.

11. Pour marinade over and marinate for 2 hours. Mix several times during this period.

12. Place hot water in wok to come within 1 inch of the bottom of round perforated steamer tray. Cover and bring to a boil over high heat to prewarm steamer. Have additional hot water on hand to replenish as necessary.

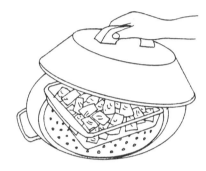

13. Reduce heat. Place dish with ribs and marinade on steamer tray. Cover and steam over slowly boiling water for 1 hour, or until ribs are tender. Periodically replenish steamer water.

14. Serve in preheated individual bowls, on white rice, if you wish.

To make about 50 to 60

2 pounds backribs, cut into bite-size pieces

Marinade:
½ teaspoon ground, roasted Szechuan peppercorns
2 teaspoons sugar
2 tablespoons light soy sauce
1 tablespoon oyster sauce
1 tablespoon Shao Hsing wine or dry sherry
¼ cup fresh orange juice
1 teaspoon sesame oil
1 fresh chili pepper, sliced
1 teaspoon minced ginger root
1 tablespoon minced garlic
2 tablespoons salted black beans
3 scallions (white part only), minced

3 tablespoons tapioca starch

MANDARIN DUMPLINGS

Saam ling gow

These shrimp-filled dumplings use the traditional har gow wrapper—a translucent wrapper made of wheat starch, tapioca starch, and lard. The wrapper is folded into a "three-cornered hat" shape for an attractive, different presentation.

1. Soak dried mushrooms in tepid water to cover for about 30 minutes, or until soft and pliable. When reconstituted, squeeze out excess water, cut off and discard stems, and mince caps.

2. Shell and devein shrimp. Place in a bowl, sprinkle with 1 teaspoon of salt, and mix well with the fingers. Rinse in several changes of cold water and drain thoroughly.

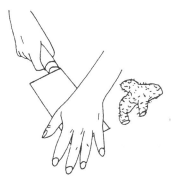

3. Break off a small piece of ginger root, peel, and mash beneath flat cleaver blade. Mince.

4. Combine all filling ingredients in a bowl. Mix thoroughly with a wooden spatula or chopsticks until smooth and tacky. Refrigerate for 2 hours.

5. Prepare har gow wrappers. Press out 3-inch-diameter disks with oiled tortilla press.

6. Soak bamboo steamer in water for about 15 minutes.

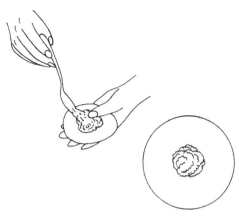

7. Spoon about 1 heaping tea-spoon of filling onto a wrapper.

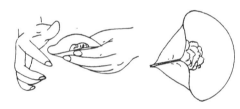

8. Fold the wrapper in half and seal ⅓ of the edge by pinching together.

9. Push the filling lightly into the pocket.

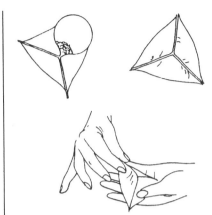

10. Take the center of the un-sealed edge with the thumb and forefinger, bring it up to sealed edge, and pinch together. This will create a three-cornered dumpling. Seal remaining two edges.

11. Make remaining dumplings. If preparing ahead, place dumplings on an oiled plate, cover with plastic wrap, and refrigerate.

12. Wipe steamer dry and lightly oil inside steamer bottom.

13. Place hot water in wok to come within 1 inch of the bottom of steamer. Boil water over high heat to preheat steamer. Have additional hot water on hand to replenish as necessary.

14. Remove steamer tray and ar-range dumplings inside, leaving space between each. Cover, return steamer to wok, and steam over rapidly boiling water for 10 minutes or until the filling is just done.

15. Serve with Soy Sauce–Chili Pepper Oil–Vinegar Dip.

To make 25 to 30

Filling:
8 medium-sized dried black Chinese mushrooms
¾ pound shrimp
1 teaspoon salt for shrimp
½ teaspoon minced ginger
½ cup minced fresh chives, preferably Chinese chives
¼ teaspoon salt
1 tablespoon light soy sauce
1 tablespoon oyster sauce
1 tablespoon Shao Hsing wine or dry sherry
1 teaspoon sesame oil
2 tablespoons tapioca starch

25 to 30 Har Gow Dough wrappers (page 100)
Oil

Soy Sauce–Chili Pepper Oil–Vinegar Dip (page 114)

RICE NOODLE ROLLS

Cheung fun

Large, flat, rice noodle skins are made by steaming a mixture of rice flour, tapioca starch, and all-purpose flour, mixed with a liberal amount of peanut oil and water. A succulent filling is rolled up in these wrappers, which are then cut to serving size.

1. Combine filling mixture in a bowl and mix well until it becomes tacky. Refrigerate for 1 hour.

2. Place wrapper batter ingredients in work bowl of food processor or blender. Process until thoroughly mixed. Empty into large bowl.

3. Lightly oil two 9- × 9-inch heavy duty cake pans and one shallow cake pan.

4. Pour ¼ cup batter into one 9- × 9-inch pan and tilt back and forth to cover the bottom entirely. Place in hot steamer and steam for 2 minutes.

5. Remove steamer lid. Place 2 tablespoons of filling in a strip about 1½ inches wide along the wrapper, as shown. Replace lid and steam for 2 more minutes.

6. Remove pan from steamer and set aside to cool for 2 or 3 minutes.

7. Stir batter well and repeat with second 9- × 9-inch pan.

8. Loosen the sides of noodle sheet in first pan. Carefully lift side nearest the filling strip and cover the filling. Roll to form a somewhat flat roll about 2 inches wide.

9. Remove roll and place on a shallow oiled cake pan, seam side down.

10. Repeat with remaining ingredients. Scrape pans clean and oil again after each use.

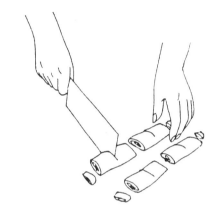

11. To serve, trim each end as necessary to make a neat roll.

12. Cut each roll in half and make a ¾-inch cut in the center of each half.

13. Place on individual plates and steam until just hot. Serve with Soy Sauce–Szechuan Peppercorn Oil Dip.

To make 12 rolls

Filling:
10 ounces coarsely
    ground chuck
10 water chestnuts,
    minced
¼ cup minced scallion
½ teaspoon minced
    ginger
½ teaspoon sugar
1 tablespoon oyster
    sauce
1 teaspoon soy sauce
½ beaten egg
1 teaspoon sesame oil
6 tablespoons chicken
    stock
3 tablespoons tapioca
    starch
1 tablespoon Shao
    Hsing wine or dry
    sherry

Wrapper:
2 cups all-purpose flour
½ cup rice flour
2 tablespoons tapioca
    starch
⅓ cup peanut oil
3 cups water
½ teaspoon salt

Soy Sauce–Szechuan
    Peppercorn Oil Dip
    (page 115)

STEAMED PEARL BALLS

Jun jew kao

This unusual deem sum variation uses rice grains, rather than a conventional dough skin, as a "wrapper." This is possible because we use glutinous rice, which becomes sticky when cooked. A pork mixture is rolled into balls that are then coated with rice grains and steamed. The glutinous rice sticks together forming an attractive, small rice ball with a succulent center of pork and spices.

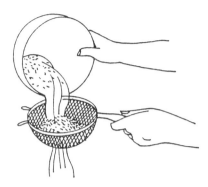

1. Put rice in a mixing bowl and wash under running water until water runs clear. Drain. Pour in 2 cups warm water and set aside for 3 hours.

2. Combine all ingredients except rice and dip. Mix thoroughly until tacky. Refrigerate for 1 hour.

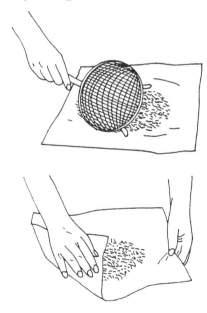

3. Drain rice. Pat dry with towel and place on a plate.

4. Soak bamboo steamer in water for about 15 minutes.

5. Lightly oil another plate with a diameter about 2 inches smaller than your steamer.

6. Place a bowl of water on worktable.

7. Dampen hand and a tablespoon with water. Take a handful of pork mixture and squeeze enough through the opening between the thumb and forefinger to form a ball about 1 inch in diameter.

8. Using the dampened spoon, improve the shape and transfer the ball to rice plate.

9. Roll ball in rice to coat.

10. Place rice-coated ball on oiled plate. Repeat with remaining pork mixture. Allow ½ inch space between balls on plate.

11. Place hot water in wok to come within 1 inch of the bottom of round perforated steamer tray. Cover and boil water over high heat to prewarm steamer. Have additional hot water on hand to replenish as necessary.

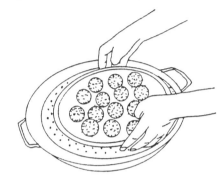

12. Place plate of rice-coated balls in hot steamer. Cover, and steam over rapidly boiling water for 20 minutes.

13. Turn heat down to mid-low and steam until rice becomes transparent (about 10 more minutes).

14. Serve hot with Soy Sauce–Chili Pepper Oil–Vinegar Dip.

To make 24

¾ cup sweet (glutinous) rice

8 ounces ground pork
1 teaspoon minced ginger
1 tablespoon minced scallion, white part only
1 whole egg plus 1 egg yolk, lightly beaten
2 teaspoons Shao Hsing wine or dry sherry
⅓ teaspoon salt mixed with 1 teaspoon light soy sauce
1 teaspoon sugar
½ teaspoon sesame oil
2 tablespoons tapioca starch
Dash white pepper

Soy Sauce–Chili Pepper Oil–Vinegar Dip (page 114)

LOTUS LEAF RICE

Naw mai gai

The original reasons for wrapping food in the large leaves of tropical plants such as the banana, ti, or lotus could have been simply utilitarian—man's first lunchbox as he was sent off to war, perhaps. Or, more likely, leaf wrappings served as a simple, available cooking container. Whatever the origins, it is clear that leaf wrappings impart to foods a special flavor that can be achieved in no other way. Lotus leaf rice is a deem sum specialty that makes superb use of this technique.

PREPARING THE RICE

1. Rinse rice in running water with many changes until water runs clear.

2. Soak rice in 2 quarts water overnight. Drain.

3. Add peanuts to 2 cups boiling water. Reduce heat to simmer. Cook 30 minutes. Drain.

4. Soak shrimp 10 minutes in cold water. Drain.

5. Heat 3 tablespoons oil in wok over medium high heat. Add drained rice and stir-fry until the rice is thoroughly coated with oil. Add peanuts, shrimp, and soy sauce. Stir-fry to mix. Remove and cool to room temperature.

6. Soak bamboo steamer in water for about 10 minutes.

7. Wipe steamer dry. Place hot water in wok to come within 1 inch of the bottom of steamer. Bring water to rapid boil. Have additional hot water on hand to replenish as necessary.

8. Place several layers of damp cheesecloth in steamer basket. Add rice mixture. Spread evenly.

9. Cover. Place steamer in wok over rapidly boiling hot water and steam for 10 minutes.

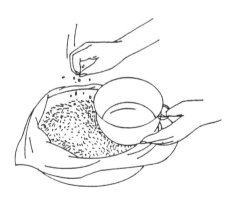

10. Place ½ cup water in small bowl. Remove steamer lid (opening away from you). Dip fingers into water and quickly sprinkle surface of rice. Use all of the water. Re-cover immediately. Repeat every 10 minutes. Replenish boiling steamer water as needed.

11. After 40 minutes test a few grains of rice at the rim of the steamer. If they are rounded and soft, the rice is done. Remove steamer from wok and let rice cool to room temperature in the basket.

PREPARING STUFFING MIXTURE

12. Toss diced chicken in marinade and let stand for 2 hours.

13. Heat 2 tablespoons oil in wok until it starts to smoke. Using the steel spatula, coat sides of wok with hot oil.

14. Add marinated chicken and stir-fry until just done. Remove and set aside.

15. Carefully clean the black coating from the preserved duck eggs. Wash under running water.

16. Hard-boil eggs. Plunge into cold water to cool.

17. When cool enough to handle, peel, and reserve yolks. Discard whites.

18. Cut each yolk in half. Refrigerate until needed.

19. Cut each sausage into 5 pieces. Set aside in small bowl.

20. Dice barbecued pork into 10 pieces. Set aside in small bowl.

21. Set aside peeled chestnuts in small bowl.

To make 10

Rice mixture:
4 cups sweet (glutinous) rice
¾ cup shelled and skinned raw peanuts
¼ cup dried shrimp
3 tablespoons oil
3 tablespoons soy sauce

Stuffing:
½ chicken breast, skinned, boned, and diced into 20 pieces

Marinade:
½ egg white
1 teaspoon soy sauce
¼ teaspoon sugar
1 teaspoon sesame oil
Pinch white pepper

2 tablespoons oil

5 salted duck eggs (optional)
4 Chinese pork sausages
½ pound Barbecued Pork (page 82)
10 chestnuts, either roasted and peeled or cooked in syrup (optional)

10 lotus leaves

41

PREPARING LOTUS LEAVES

22. Soak the leaves in cold water until pliable. Wash thoroughly.

23. Bring 3 to 4 quarts water to boil in a large pot. Add leaves and boil for 10 minutes. Drain and soak in a large container of salted water for 20 minutes.

24. Drain. Pat dry with towel.

PREPARING THE SAUCE

25. Combine chicken stock, hoisin sauce, oyster sauce, soy sauce, sugar, wine, cornstarch, and pepper in a small bowl.

26. Heat 2 tablespoons oil in wok until it begins to smoke. Coat sides of wok with hot oil.

27. Add ginger and stir-fry for a couple of seconds. Add pork and stir-fry until it turns white and separates.

28. Stir seasonings to make sure cornstarch is fully dissolved. Add to pork. Stir-fry until mixture thickens.

29. Mix in chicken, pork sausage, and barbecued pork. Stir to blend. Set aside to cool, or refrigerate until ready to wrap.

ASSEMBLY AND STEAMING

30. Organize the following ingredients on the worktable:

Stack of lotus leaves
Rice
Meat and chicken mixture
Hardboiled duck egg yolks
Chestnuts
Bowl of water

31. Divide rice into 10 portions.

32. Spread a leaf, folded in half, in front of you. Cut stem off.

33. With wet hands, divide a rice portion in half and spread one half on a 4- × 4-inch area on the leaf.

34. Place a tenth of the meat and chicken mixture in the center of the rice.

35. Add half an egg yolk and 1 chestnut.

36. Cover with the second half-portion of rice.

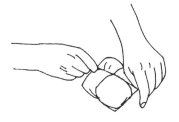

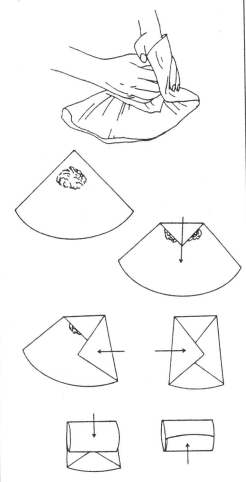

37. Fold the leaf over as shown to make a tight package.

38. Tie with kitchen string (optional).

39. Repeat procedure to fill and fold all lotus leaves.

40. Steam over rapidly boiling water for 15 minutes.

41. Serve hot. Lotus leaf rice may be frozen and resteamed for 45 minutes to serve.

Sauce:
½ cup Chicken Stock (page 116)
2 teaspoons hoisin sauce
1 teaspoon oyster sauce
1 teaspoon soy sauce
1 teaspoon sugar
1 tablespoon Shao Hsing wine or dry sherry
1 tablespoon cornstarch
Pinch white pepper
2 tablespoons oil
1 teaspoon minced ginger root
4 ounces ground pork

SHRIMP GOLDFISH

Gum yue gow

Deem sum can awaken your decorative instincts. Wrappers can be shaped into birds, flowers, fishes, rabbits—even frogs. Here, the lowly dumpling is transformed into an elegant goldfish with flowing tail.

1. Combine filling ingredients and mix thoroughly. Refrigerate for 2 hours.

2. Prepare har gow wrappers. Press out 3-inch disks on a lightly oiled tortilla press.

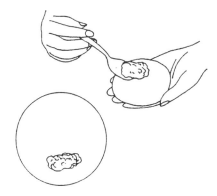

3. Place a tablespoon of filling on a wrapper, slightly off center.

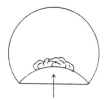

4. Fold the edge closest to the filling up and over the filling.

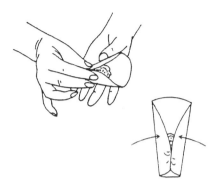

5. Fold each side up and pinch center.

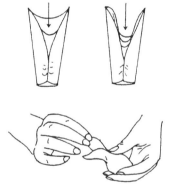

6. Fold opposite end into filling. Pinch to form the tail.

7. Dye the eyes with food coloring.

8. Soak bamboo steamer in water for about 10 minutes. Dry and lightly oil each compartment bottom. Place hot water in wok to come within 1 inch of bottom of steamer. Boil water over high heat. Have additional water on hand to replenish if necessary.

9. Arrange goldfish on steamer rack leaving space between each. Cover and steam for 15 minutes.

10. Serve with Soy Sauce–Szechuan Peppercorn Oil Dip.

To make 30

Filling:
8 ounces shrimp, shelled, deveined, cleaned, and minced
½ cup minced bamboo shoots
2 tablespoons minced scallion, white part only
2 tablespoons minced coriander
2 tablespoons finely minced pork fat
½ teaspoon minced ginger
2 teaspoons light soy sauce
1 teaspoon sugar
⅛ teaspoon salt
1 teaspoon sesame oil
¼ teaspoon white pepper
2 teaspoons tapioca starch
1 tablespoon Shao Hsing wine or dry sherry
30 Har Gow Dough wrappers (page 100)
Oil

Red food coloring

Soy Sauce–Szechuan Peppercorn Oil Dip (page 115)

DEEP-FRIED DISHES

SHRIMP TOAST

Har dor see

The Yank Sing recipe for shrimp toast is a variation of the conventional in that it uses a whole shrimp with tail left attached. This creates a more decorative and tasty deem sum than you would produce by using the shrimp paste alone.

1. Warm oven to 140°F. or lowest temperature.

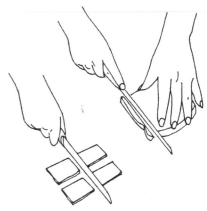

2. Cut the crusts from the bread. Cut the bread into 24 1¼- × 2-inch pieces. Spread all the bread including crusts and leftover pieces out on cookie sheet.

3. Set bread in oven to dry for 1 to 1½ hours. Turn pieces over at half-way point.

4. Reserve 24 shrimp. Shell, devein, and clean the rest. Set aside.

5. Shell, devein, and clean the remaining 24 shrimp, leaving the tails attached.

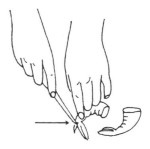

6. Cut away the triangular tip as shown. (This tip contains water and will pop in the oil when fried.)

7. Slice the 24 shrimp almost in half lengthwise so they may be opened and flattened out. Place them in a bowl with marinade, cover, and refrigerate for 1 hour.

8. Mince the remaining shrimp fine. Using the back of a Chinese cleaver, chop into a fine mash.

9. Prepare the rest of the ingredients. Add to a bowl with the shrimp and mix together until tacky. Cover and refrigerate until ready to use.

10. Remove bread from the oven. Roll the crusts and leftover pieces between two sheets of wax paper to make breadcrumbs.

11. Pat dry the marinated whole shrimp with paper towel.

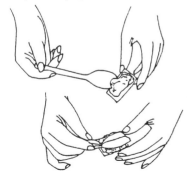

12. Spread a teaspoon of shrimp paste onto a bread wafer, covering the surface. Press a butterflied shrimp onto the paste, cut side down.

13. Spread a heaping teaspoon of shrimp paste evenly on top. Sprinkle with breadcrumbs. Prepare all of the shrimp in this manner.

14. Neatly arrange shrimp toast, paper toweling or wire rack, and utensils such as wire mesh strainer, cooking chopsticks, and the like around the cooking area. Be sure your wok cover and extinguisher are handy in case of an oil fire.

15. Pour 6 cups of oil into wok. Attach deep-frying thermometer and heat over medium heat to 325°F.

16. Gently add a shrimp toast (shrimp side down) to the oil and fry until golden brown, about 3 to 4 minutes. It should not be necessary to turn the shrimp toast over to fry the bread. Remove and sample. The shrimp should be cooked. The bread wafer should be golden brown, and not oily or greasy. Adjust your time and temperature and fry the remaining shrimp toast in small quantities, replacing one each time one is removed from the oil.

17. Drain on a wire rack or paper toweling. Shrimp toast may be served immediately, or made earlier and reheated in a preheated 350°F. oven for 5 minutes.

To make 24

6 thin slices white bread
1 pound shrimp (about 40 to 50 count)

Marinade:
⅛ teaspoon salt
2 teaspoons Shao Hsing wine or dry sherry
½ egg white, lightly beaten

2 tablespoons pork fat
3 tablespoons minced scallion, white part only
8 water chestnuts, minced
1 teaspoon ginger juice
1 tablespoon Shao Hsing wine or dry sherry
¼ teaspoon salt
1 teaspoon sugar
1 teaspoon sesame oil
1 teaspoon oyster sauce
⅛ teaspoon white pepper
½ teaspoon light soy sauce
1 egg white, lightly beaten
4 teaspoons tapioca starch or cornstarch

Oil for deep-frying

CHICKEN LOLLIPOPS

Yeung gai yik

Chicken lollipops are surely the definitive "finger food." The meat on the wing is scraped forward and inverted over the large joint end, providing a small bundle of heavenly chicken thoughtfully equipped with its own handle.

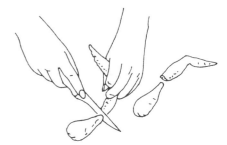

1. Cut the meat from the chicken wings. Save the wing tip parts for the stockpot or use with another recipe.

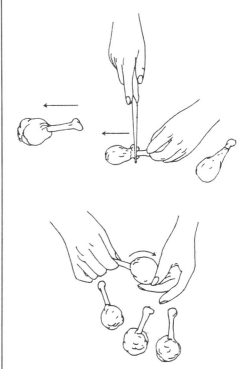

2. Separate the bone from the meat by pushing it toward the large end. Invert over the end (leaving it attached), forming a ball of meat.

3. Combine marinade ingredients in a large bowl. Add chicken, mix thoroughly, and marinate for 20 minutes.

4. Partially mix batter ingredients together in a bowl. For best results, the batter should not be thoroughly mixed, which would create an unappetizing dough casing around the meat when fried. A partially mixed batter with some undissolved flour will give a light, crispy coating.

5. Conveniently arrange chicken wings to be fried, bowl of flour, bowl of batter, paper toweling or wire rack, and utensils such as wire mesh strainer and cooking chopsticks around the cooking area. Be sure your wok cover and extinguisher are handy in case of an oil fire.

6. Add 6 cups of oil to wok, attach deep-frying thermometer, and heat over medium heat to slightly above cooking temperature of 375°F.

7. Coat only the meat portion, not the bone, of marinated chicken lightly with flour and dip into batter. Let drain momentarily over the bowl.

8. Gently insert in the oil and fry until golden brown, about 3 to 4 minutes. Remove and sample. The meat should be just done. The exterior crust should be golden brown, and not oily or greasy. Adjust your time and temperature and fry the remaining chicken pieces a few at a time, replacing a piece each time one is removed from the oil.

9. Drain on a wire rack or paper toweling. Serve hot. Chicken Lollipops may be frozen and reheated (undefrosted) in a 425°F. oven for 15 minutes. Or they may be defrosted and refried at 375°F. just long enough to heat through.

To make 30

30 small chicken wings

Marinade:
2 teaspoons minced
   ginger root
2 tablespoons minced
   scallion, white part
   only
¼ cup minced coriander
2 teaspoons minced
   garlic
3 tablespoons soy
   sauce
2 teaspoons Shao Hsing
   wine or dry sherry
½ teaspoon sesame oil

Batter:
½ cup all-purpose flour
⅓ cup cold water
1 egg, beaten

Flour for dusting
Oil for deep-frying

SPRING ROLLS

Cheun guen

Year in and year out at Yank Sing, spring rolls continue to be one of the most popular deem sum. This is no less true in China, where they are a New Year's treat. You remember, of course, that Chinese New Year is celebrated in February, hence the name "spring" rolls. Their popularity has a great deal to do with the spring roll wrapper, which is a crêpelike skin that fries to a very light, crispy envelope.

1. Combine the marinade ingredients. Add shredded pork and mix well. Cover and marinate for 2 hours in the refrigerator.

2. Soak dried mushrooms in tepid water to cover for about 30 minutes, or until soft and pliable. When reconstituted, squeeze out water. Cut off and discard stems, and mince caps.

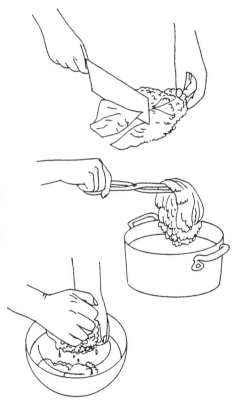

3. Cut away white part of Chinese cabbage. Blanch green part in boiling water for 1 minute. Plunge in bowl of cold water to halt cooking. Drain and squeeze out excess water.

4. Cut leaves into 1-inch strips lengthwise and shred to make about 1 cup. Set aside.

5. Prepare remaining filling ingredients, arranging them separately on a work platter.

6. Heat 2 tablespoons oil in wok over medium heat. Using the steel spatula, coat the sides of the wok with hot oil.

7. Stir-fry ginger and garlic for about 10 seconds. Turn heat up high and add marinated pork. Stir-fry until pork turns white.

8. Add shrimp and stir-fry until pink.

9. Add mushrooms, bamboo shoots, scallion, and Chinese cabbage. Stir-fry for 2 more minutes.

10. Add chicken stock.

11. Add cornstarch-water mixture and continue to stir-fry until liquid thickens.

12. Spread filling on plate to cool to room temperature.

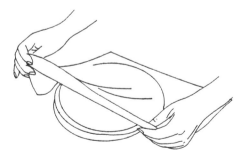

13. Keep spring roll skins under a damp towel. Remove one skin and place it on the work surface.

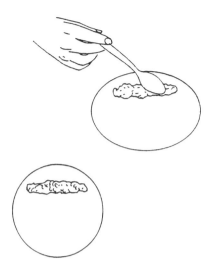

14. Place about 2 tablespoons of stuffing on the skin about 1 inch from the edge nearest you.

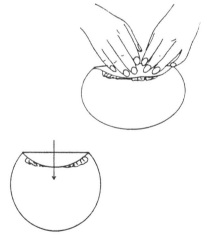

15. Fold the near edge over the filling.

To make 20

Marinade:
¼ teaspoon salt
2 teaspoons soy sauce
2 teaspoons oyster sauce
1 tablespoon Shao Hsing wine or dry sherry
1 teaspoon sugar
Pinch white pepper
½ teaspoon sesame oil
2 teaspoons cornstarch

Filling:
8 ounces pork, shredded
8 dried black Chinese mushrooms
5 Chinese cabbage leaves, green part only
½ teaspoon minced ginger root
½ teaspoon minced garlic
4 ounces shrimp, shelled, deveined, cleaned, and shredded
½ cup shredded bamboo shoots
¼ cup shredded scallion
¼ cup Chicken Stock (page 116)
1 tablespoon cornstarch mixed with 1 tablespoon water

2 tablespoons oil
20 spring roll skins
1 egg, lightly beaten
Oil for deep-frying

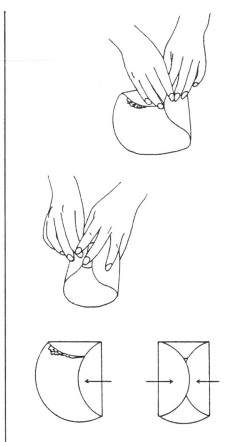

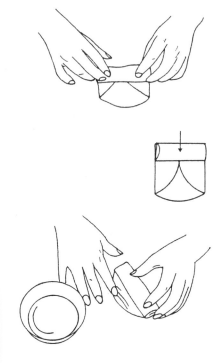

16. Fold over the right and left sides.

17. Roll up and seal with beaten egg.

18. Set aside, sealed side down, covered with plastic wrap. Continue with the remaining ingredients. Spring rolls may be refrigerated or frozen at this point until ready to fry.

19. Arrange spring rolls, paper toweling or wire rack, and utensils such as wire mesh strainer and cooking chopsticks in convenient fashion around the cooking area. Be sure your wok cover and extinguisher are handy in case of an oil fire.

20. Add 6 cups of oil to wok. Attach deep-frying thermometer and heat to slightly above cooking temperature of 375°F.

21. Add a spring roll to the oil and fry until golden brown, about 3 to 4 minutes. Turn several times while frying. Remove and sample. The interior filling should be heated through. The exterior crust should be golden brown, and not oily or greasy. Adjust your time and temperature and fry the remaining spring rolls a few at a time, replacing one each time one is removed from the oil.

22. Drain on a wire rack or paper toweling. Just before serving, you may want to cut the spring rolls into 3 or 4 bite-size pieces with kitchen scissors. Serve hot or at room temperature.

TARO DUMPLINGS

Woo gok

Taro is a starchy, white-fleshed tuber available in oriental and Latin markets. To make these dumplings, pork filling is wrapped in taro dough and deep-fried. Deep-frying produces a crunchy surface crust which contrasts nicely with the soft interior. When filling the dumplings, watch out for thin spots in the dough, which may cause the dumpling to burst when fried.

1. Soak dried mushrooms in tepid water to cover for about 30 minutes, or until soft and pliable. When reconstituted, squeeze out excess water, cut off and discard stems, and mince caps.

2. Shell and devein shrimp. Place in a bowl, sprinkle with 1 teaspoon of salt and mix well with fingers. Rinse in several changes of cold water and drain thoroughly and mince.

3. Prepare remaining filling ingredients and mix, together with minced mushrooms and shrimp, in a bowl until tacky. (A garlic press is useful for squeezing the juice from a small piece of ginger.)

4. Refrigerate for 2 hours.

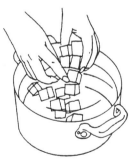

5. Peel taro root and cut into ½-inch slices. Put in a pan and just cover with water. Boil gently until tender when pierced with chopstick, about 1 hour. Replenish water as necessary to cover taro.

6. Drain well. Reserve liquid.

7. Mash taro root to the consistency of mashed potatoes. Eliminate all lumps. Set aside.

8. Place wheat starch in bowl of food processor or blender.

9. Measure 1 cup reserved taro liquid. (Add water to make 1 cup if necessary.) Bring to boil in saucepan.

10. Turn on processor and add boiling liquid through feed tube. Process to a thick liquid. (This may be done by hand in a mixing bowl by pouring the liquid with one hand while mixing with the other. Smooth, lump-free results are more easily achieved with the processor, however.)

11. Add wheat starch mixture to mashed taro. Add lard, sugar, salt, and five-spice powder. Mix with wooden spatula until mixture is thoroughly blended.

12. Refrigerate for 2 to 4 hours. Note: Refrigeration will firm the mixture to handling consistency.

13. Heat 2 tablespoons oil in wok and stir-fry filling mixture until pork turns white, about 4 to 5 minutes.

14. Empty onto plate and cool to room temperature. Refrigerate until ready to use.

15. Divide taro dough into 20 lemon-size balls. Have a bowl of water standing by. Wet fingers. Form one ball into cup shape.

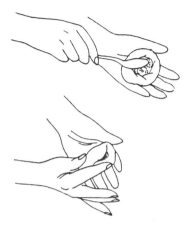

16. Place a heaping tablespoon (about a twentieth) of filling mixture in cavity and close opening.

17. Form into egg shape between palms. Repeat with remaining ingredients.

18. Arrange dumplings to be fried, paper toweling or drain rack, and utensils such as wire mesh strainer and cooking chopsticks conveniently around cooking area. Be sure your wok cover and extinguisher are handy in case of an oil fire.

19. Add 6 cups of oil to wok. Attach deep-fry thermometer and heat oil to slightly above cooking temperature of 350°F.

20. Gently add a taro dumpling to the oil and fry until golden brown and heated through. Remove and sample. Adjust your time and temperature and cook the remaining dumplings three or four at a time, replacing one each time one is removed from the oil.

21. Drain on a wire rack or paper toweling. Serve hot.

To make 20

Filling:
6 medium-sized dried
  Chinese black
  mushrooms
6 ounces shrimp
1 teaspoon fresh ginger
  juice
8 ounces pork butt,
  coarsely minced
¾ teaspoon sugar
1¾ teaspoons salt
½ teaspoon sesame oil
2 teaspoons oyster
  sauce
1 teaspoon soy sauce
1 tablespoon Shao
  Hsing wine or dry
  sherry
1 tablespoon tapioca
  starch
1 egg white

Taro dough:
1½ pounds fresh taro
1 cup wheat starch
⅔ cup lard, softened
1 tablespoon sugar
1 teaspoon salt
1 teaspoon five-spice
  powder

2 tablespoons oil
Oil for deep-frying

SWEET RICE DUMPLINGS

Haam suey gok

Sweet rice dumplings combine a crispy fried exterior; a soft, slightly sticky, slightly sweet, glutinous rice wrapping; and a flavorful barbecued pork filling that is a gastronomic triple play. If you have ever enjoyed these wonderful dumplings in a Chinatown teahouse, you will covet the following recipe.

1. Dice barbecued pork to small pea size. Set aside.

2. Soak dried mushrooms in tepid water to cover for about 30 minutes, or until soft and pliable. When reconstituted, squeeze out excess water, cut off and discard stems, mince caps coarsely, and set aside.

3. Soak dried shrimp in water to cover for about 10 minutes. Mince coarsely. Set aside.

4. Combine sauce ingredients in a small bowl. Set aside.

5. Heat 3 tablespoons oil in wok over high heat. Add scallions. Stir-fry 20 seconds. Add mushrooms, shrimp, bamboo shoots, water chestnuts, and barbecued pork. Stir-fry for 1 minute or until heated through.

6. Stir sauce with chopsticks to circulate cornstarch and pour into wok. Stir-fry until sauce thickens.

7. Remove filling to a plate, cool to room temperature, and refrigerate for 2 hours.

8. Prepare sweet rice dough and refrigerate as instructed.

9. Remove dough and filling mixture from the refrigerator. Divide dough in half. Keep one half covered with plastic wrap.

10. Knead the dough a few times and roll into a cylinder 16 inches long.

11. Cut into 16 equal pieces. Roll each piece into a ball between the palms. Repeat with other half of dough.

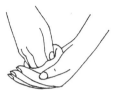

12. Shape a ball into a shallow cup. The edges of the cup should be slightly thinner than the center.

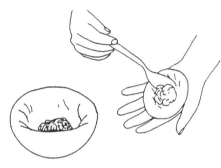

13. Spoon a tablespoon of the filling into center of dough.

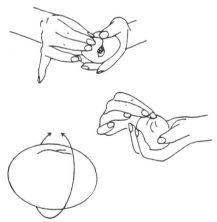

14. Bring up the sides and pinch to seal. Roll in the palms to make an egg shape. Place on slightly oiled plate. Repeat with remaining ingredients.

15. In an orderly manner around the cooking area, arrange dumplings to be fried, paper toweling or wire rack, and utensils such as wire mesh strainer and cooking chopsticks. Be sure your wok cover and extinguisher are handy in case of an oil fire.

16. Pour 6 cups of oil into wok. Attach deep-frying thermometer and heat over medium heat to slightly above cooking temperature of 350°F.

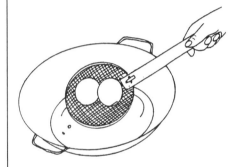

17. Add a dumpling to the oil and cook until golden brown, about 5 to 6 minutes. Turn frequently for even browning. Remove and sample. The interior filling should be heated through. The exterior crust should be golden brown, and not oily or greasy. Adjust your time and temperature and cook the remaining pastries three or four at a time, replacing a pastry each time one is removed from the oil. Turn frequently.

18. Drain pastries on a wire rack or paper toweling. Can be served either hot or at room temperature.

To make 32

Filling:
10 ounces Barbecued Pork (page 82)
10 dried black Chinese mushrooms
2 tablespoons dried shrimp
¼ cup minced scallions, green part only
4 ounces bamboo shoots, coarsely minced
16 water chestnuts, coarsely minced

Sauce:
½ teaspoon ginger juice
1½ tablespoons oyster sauce
2 teaspoons soy sauce
1 teaspoon sugar
1 teaspoon sesame oil
¼ teaspoon ground, roasted Szechuan peppercorns (see recipe for Steamed Spareribs, page 32, step 2)
1 tablespoon Shao Hsing wine or dry sherry
1½ tablespoons cornstarch
¼ cup Chicken Stock (page 116)

3 tablespoons oil
Sweet Rice Dough (page 108)
Oil for deep-frying

BEAN CURD SKIN ROLLS

San juk guen

Thin sheets of dried bean curd are used as the wrappers for this delicious deem sum. The wrapped pork, shrimp, and mushroom filling is first deep-fried and then steamed, creating a delightful combination of textures. The result is a crunchy, soft, wonderfully flavorful package that is served in its own steamed juices.

1. Prepare marinade and marinate pork for 30 minutes.

2. Heat ¼ cup oil in wok. Coat sides with oil. Add garlic, ginger, and marinated pork. Stir-fry a couple of minutes or until pork turns white. Add shredded mushrooms, shrimp, and bamboo shoots. Stir-fry until shrimp turn pink. Remove mixture and cool to room temperature.

3. Soak bean curd skins in water until pliable, about 5 minutes.

4. Drain and cut into 5- × 5-inch squares (handle gently). A 5- × 5-inch square can be made up of overlapped smaller pieces if necessary. Leftover bean curd can be used in soup, salad, or braised with some meat or vegetables.

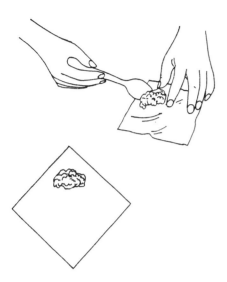

5. Place a tablespoon of filling on corner of bean curd skin. Spread to 3 inches long.

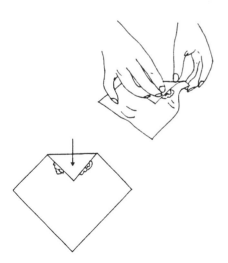

6. Fold the near corner over the filling.

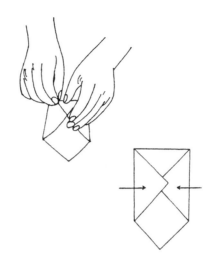

7. Fold the right and left sides toward the center.

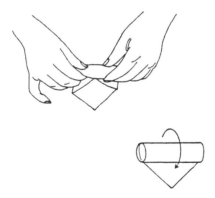

8. Roll up almost to the end.

To make 24

Marinade:
¼ cup minced scallion
¼ cup minced coriander
½ teaspoon sugar
¼ teaspoon salt
1 tablespoon soy sauce
1 tablespoon oyster
  sauce
2 tablespoons Shao
  Hsing wine or dry
  sherry
1 teaspoon sesame oil
2 teaspoons cornstarch

Filling:
¼ cup oil
1 teaspoon minced
  garlic
1 teaspoon minced
  ginger
8 ounces pork loin,
  sliced thin and
  shredded
8 ounces dried black
  Chinese mushrooms,
  reconstituted, stems
  removed, and thinly
  shredded
8 ounces shrimp,
  shelled, deveined,
  cleaned, and diced
1 cup shredded bamboo
  shoots

Enough bean curd skins
  to make 24 five-inch-
  square sheets
1 egg yolk, lightly beaten
Oil for deep-frying

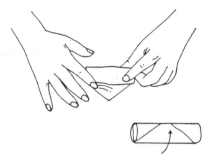

9. Dip finger in beaten egg yolk. Wet edge of last corner to seal.

10. Repeat until all skins are rolled up. Place on plate, sealed side down.

11. Refrigerate for 1 hour, uncovered.

12. Arrange bean curd rolls to be fried, paper toweling or wire rack, and utensils such as wire mesh strainer and cooking chopsticks conveniently around the frying area. Be sure your wok cover and extinguisher are handy in case of an oil fire.

13. Add 6 cups of oil to wok. Attach deep-fry thermometer and heat over medium heat to slightly above cooking temperature of 350°F.

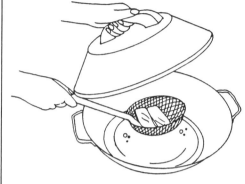

14. Add a bean curd roll to the oil and cook until golden brown, about 3 to 4 minutes. (Because of its moisture content, the bean curd roll is likely to cause a great deal of spattering. The wok cover, held like a shield, is good protection until things calm down.)

15. Remove and sample. The interior filling should be cooked. The bean curd crust should be light golden brown, and not oily or greasy. Adjust your time and temperature and cook the remaining bean curd rolls three or four at a time, replacing one each time one is removed from the oil.

16. Drain on a wire rack or paper toweling. Bean curd rolls may be served at this point; however, we would suggest coating them in the sauce and steaming for a delightful change.

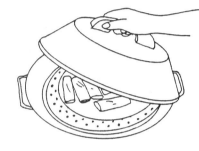

17. Combine sauce ingredients in a small saucepan and cook, stirring constantly, until the sauce thickens.

18. Dip the fried bean curd skin rolls in sauce to coat. Place on plate and steam for 5 minutes. Serve hot.

Sauce:
1 cup Chicken Stock (page 116)
2 tablespoons Shao-Hsing wine or dry sherry
1 teaspoon ginger juice
1 tablespoon oyster sauce
½ teaspoon sugar
1 teaspoon soy sauce
Pinch salt
1 teaspoon sesame oil
1 tablespoon cornstarch

FRIED FISH BALLS

Jar yue yuen

A light, flavorful fish mixture is formed into small balls and deep-fried. Just before serving, the fish balls are added to sauce, cooked gently until warmed through, and served in the sauce in individual serving bowls.

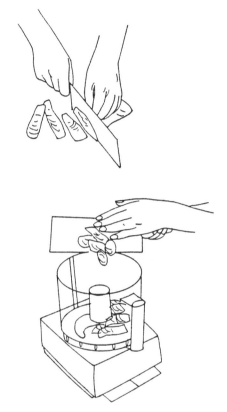

1. Put fish ball ingredients, except egg and egg yolk, in food processor with metal blade attached. Process 1 minute. Scrape down sides of bowl with spatula. Add egg and egg yolk. Process additional 15 seconds. If there are still lumps of fish remaining, process a few seconds more, but do not overprocess.

2. Arrange the processor bowl, paper toweling or wire rack, and utensils such as wire mesh strainer and cooking chopsticks around the frying area. Be sure your wok cover and extinguisher are handy in case of an oil fire.

3. Pour 6 cups of oil in wok. Attach deep-fry thermometer and heat over medium heat to slightly above cooking temperature of 350°F.

4. Oil palm of hand and a tablespoon. Place a handful of fish mixture in oiled palm.

5. Squeeze some of the mixture through the opening made by thumb and forefinger.

6. Using the oiled spoon, shape this into a 1-inch ball. Scoop it up with the spoon.

7. Gently lower it into the hot oil. Fry until golden brown, about 3 to 4 minutes. Remove and sample. The fish mixture should be cooked. The exterior crust should be golden brown, and not oily or greasy. Adjust your time and temperature and cook the remaining fish balls six or eight at a time, replacing a few each time some are removed from the oil.

8. Drain on a wire rack or paper toweling.

9. To make sauce, heat oil in saucepan. Add crushed garlic, scallions, and ginger, and brown. Discard garlic, scallions, and ginger. Turn heat off and let oil cool slightly.

10. Combine the rest of the sauce ingredients in small bowl and stir to incorporate cornstarch. Add to the oil in pan. Heat while stirring until sauce thickens.

11. Just before serving, heat sauce and add fish balls. Gently cook until fish balls are heated through. Serve in small individual bowls with sauce.

To make 40

Fish balls:
1 pound white-fleshed fish, diced
2 tablespoons chopped scallion, white part only
2 tablespoons Shao Hsing wine or dry sherry
2 teaspoons sesame oil
2 teaspoons ginger juice
2 tablespoons minced pork fat
½ teaspoon salt
1 teaspoon sugar
⅛ teaspoon white pepper
6 tablespoons tapioca starch
2 tablespoons Chicken Stock (page 116)
1 large egg plus 1 egg yolk

Oil for deep-frying

Sauce:
2 tablespoons oil
1 clove garlic, crushed
3 scallions, white part only, crushed
½-inch slice ginger, crushed
½ teaspoon sugar
1½ cups chicken stock
2 tablespoons Shao Hsing wine or dry sherry
1 tablespoon oyster sauce
1 tablespoon soy sauce
2 teaspoons sesame oil
2 teaspoons cornstarch

SILVER WRAPPED CHICKEN

Jee bow gai

Chicken thighs are marinated in several sauces and herbs, wrapped in foil, and then deep-fried. The result is a plateful of little silver surprises for your guests to open and enjoy. To keep the portions small, the thighs are cut in half. This is an easy operation if you have a Chinese cleaver and a resolute swing. The thigh should be halved in one clean stroke, otherwise the bone will splinter. If this seems difficult, the thighs may be boned before marinating. But the bone adds good flavor, so leave it in if possible.

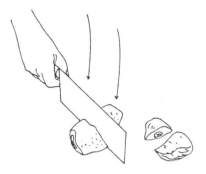

1. With a Chinese cleaver, chop chicken thighs in half through bone.

2. Blend marinade ingredients together.

3. Place chicken in a large bowl and pour marinade over. Mix well to coat each chicken piece. Cover or place in sealable plastic bag and refrigerate for 24 to 48 hours.

4. Place a piece of chicken and a teaspoon of marinade in the center of a foil square.

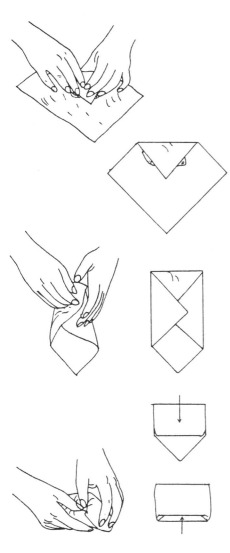

5. Wrap chicken as shown.

6. Heat about 6 cups of oil for deep-frying to 350°F.

7. Deep-fry the wrapped chicken packages a few at a time for about 7 to 10 minutes. Serve warm.

To make 24

12 chicken thighs (about
  4 pounds)

Marinade:
¼ cup ground bean
  sauce
3 tablespoons hoisin
  sauce
1 tablespoon plum
  sauce
5 tablespoons soy
  sauce
2 tablespoons Shao
  Hsing wine or dry
  sherry
2 tablespoons sesame
  oil
2 teaspoons minced
  garlic
4 teaspoons minced
  ginger root
¼ cup (packed) minced
  scallions
¼ cup (packed) minced
  coriander
⅓ teaspoon five-spice
  powder
⅛ teaspoon ground
  white pepper
1½ teaspoons salt
½ cup sugar

24 nine-inch square
  pieces heavy-duty foil
Oil for deep-frying

CREAM CHEESE WONTON

"Cheese" Wun tun

The number of different fillings for wonton probably roughly equals the number of different Chinese cooks. Yank Sing has had great success with a cream cheese filling mixed with a little curry powder. We are including instructions for making the skins at home. However, excellent, thin wonton skins are packaged and readily available in the markets. The advantage to making the skins at home is that you can improve the flavor by adding more eggs than you would customarily find in the commercial product.

1. Mash cream cheese in a bowl with fork until smooth. Add egg yolks and curry powder. Mix until completely lump-free. Set aside. If time allows, refrigerate for 2 hours for easier handling.

2. Combine sweet-sour dip ingredients in a saucepan and cook over medium heat while stirring constantly until sauce thickens. Set aside.

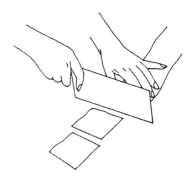

3. Prepare Wonton Skins (page 110).

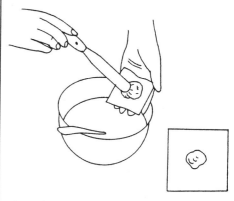

4. Place a teaspoon of cream cheese mixture on a wrapper.

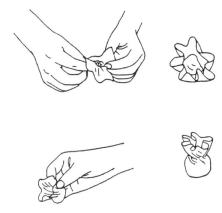

5. Gather up the edges and pinch to enclose. Set aside on a cookie sheet. Repeat with remainder.

6. Heat 6 cups of oil in wok to 350°F.

7. Fry 5 or 6 wonton at a time for 3 to 4 seconds or until light golden brown. They will puff up so don't fry too many at once.

8. Remove and drain on wire rack or paper toweling.

9. Serve with warm dipping sauce.

To make about 100

Filling:
8 ounces cream cheese, at room temperature
2 egg yolks
1 teaspoon curry powder

Sweet-sour dip:
1½ cups unsweetened pineapple juice
½ cup distilled white vinegar
¾ cup sugar
3 tablespoons catsup
3 tablespoons cornstarch

Wonton wrappers
Oil for deep-frying

STUFFED CRAB CLAWS

Yeung hai keem

There is no question about it, crab claws are attention-getters. But they are also delicious hors d'oeuvres, with the exposed claw providing a convenient handle. The shells are partially removed, exposing the meat. The claws are steamed and then enclosed in a paste of shrimp and crabmeat. They are then coated in flour, eggs, and breadcrumbs, and briefly deep-fried.

1. Chop shrimp coarsely and place in work bowl of food processor with metal blade attached. Process until almost a paste but still retaining some texture. Empty into large bowl. Add remaining filling ingredients and mix until pasty. Refrigerate for 2 hours.

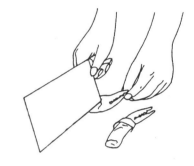

2. Using the cleaver, crack and remove about ⅔ of the crab claw shell, exposing the meat.

3. Preheat a steamer. Place claws on a plate and steam for 10 minutes. Cool to room temperature.

4. Heat 6 cups of oil in wok to 350°F.

5. Line up crab claws, bowl of water, filling mixture, flour, beaten egg, and breadcrumbs neatly near cooking area.

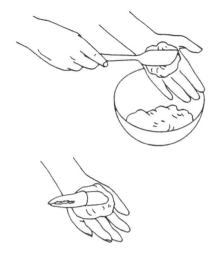

6. Wet one hand. Scoop up ½ of filling mixture onto palm. Place crab claw on top and coat it with filling.

7. Dip crab claw into flour.

8. Dry hand and smoothly mold claw. Dip in beaten egg and then in breadcrumbs.

9. Repeat with two more claws.

10. Gently put coated claws into hot oil. Deep-fry for 4 minutes, turning occasionally. Remove when golden brown. Drain on wire rack or paper towel.

11. Repeat with remaining ingredients, three claws at a time. Serve warm with Mustard–Soy Sauce Dip.

To make 12

Filling:
8 ounces shrimp, shelled, deveined, and cleaned
8 ounces cooked crabmeat, finely minced
1 tablespoon finely minced pork fat
1 teaspoon ginger juice
2 teaspoons oyster sauce
1 teaspoon sugar
½ teaspoon salt
2 teaspoons Shao Hsing wine or dry sherry
Pinch white pepper
½ egg white, lightly beaten
1 teaspoon sesame oil
2 tablespoons tapioca starch
½ cup flour

12 crab claws

½ cup flour
1 large egg beaten with 1 tablespoon water

Breadcrumbs
Oil for deep-frying

Mustard–Soy Sauce Dip (page 115)

71

PAN-FRIED DISHES

POT STICKERS

War teep

Pot stickers are cooked by a combination of pan-frying and steaming. Employing these two radically different cooking methods results in a dumpling that is soft and tender on the top and crisply fried on the bottom. The traditional dip is a combination of chili pepper oil and white vinegar mixed to taste by each guest.

1. Soak dried mushrooms in tepid water to cover for about 30 minutes, or until soft and pliable. When reconstituted, squeeze out excess water, cut off and discard stems, and mince caps.

2. Place ground pork in bowl. Add mushrooms, scallion, ginger, and chicken stock. Mix well.

3. Add remaining filling ingredients except Chinese cabbage and salt. Mix until tacky. Cover and refrigerate for 2 hours.

4. Place chopped cabbage in bowl and sprinkle with salt. Mix by hand and set aside for 10 minutes.

5. Place cabbage in kitchen towel and squeeze out excess water. Set aside.

6. Prepare pot sticker wrappers.

7. Mix reserved cabbage into filling mixture just before making dumplings.

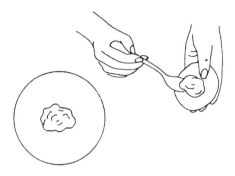

8. Place a heaping teaspoon of filling on a wrapper.

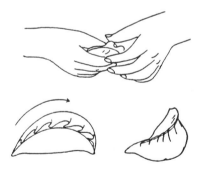

9. Fold in half, making a half-moon shape.

10. Starting from one end, pleat one edge of the dough in an overlapping fashion and pinch to other to seal. The shape should be a slightly off center crescent. At this point, pot stickers may be frozen for later cooking.

11. Heat a heavy frying pan to hot over medium heat and coat bottom with 1 tablespoon oil.

12. Off heat, arrange dumplings in pan flat side down, allowing space between each.

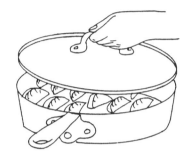

13. Fry dumplings at medium heat until bottoms turn light golden brown. Pour in hot water, cover immediately, and cook for 5 to 6 minutes. All water should evaporate.

14. Pour in remaining 2 tablespoons of oil (do not pour onto dumplings). Fry uncovered until the undersides of dumplings are golden brown and crisp.

15. Serve with Soy Sauce–Chili Pepper Oil–Vinegar Dip.

To make about 36

Filling:
4 dried black Chinese mushrooms
8 ounces ground pork
¼ cup minced scallion
1 teaspoon minced ginger root
2 tablespoons Chicken Stock (page 116)
1 large egg, beaten
2 teaspoons soy sauce
1 teaspoon sesame oil
⅛ teaspoon ground white pepper
2 teaspoons oyster sauce
1 tablespoon Shao Hsing wine or dry sherry
2 cups finely chopped Chinese cabbage
1 teaspoon salt

36 Pot Sticker Wrappers (page 102)
3 tablespoons oil
½ cup hot water

Soy Sauce–Chili Pepper Oil–Vinegar Dip (page 114)

TURNIP CAKES

Law bak go

There is a slight problem with nomenclature here. This delicious little vegetable cake is universally known as a turnip cake, but (in California, at least) it is always made with the Japanese daikon, an elongated radish. To further complicate matters, the daikon is often called a Chinese turnip! So round and round we go. Nomenclature aside, the daikon is finely shredded and mixed with rice flour and a variety of other tasty things to form a paste. This is steamed, then cut into cakes and pan-fried. It should be served hot, with a little soy sauce and chili oil for a dip.

1. Soak dried mushrooms in tepid water to cover for about 30 minutes, or until soft and pliable. When reconstituted, cut off and discard stems. Mince caps coarsely.

2. Soak dried shrimp in ¼ cup tepid water for about 10 minutes. Drain. Reserve liquid. Mince coarsely.

3. Mince pork sausage.

4. Peel daikon and shred. A processor with shredding attachment is useful here.

5. Place shredded daikon in a saucepan. Add chicken stock and reserved shrimp liquid. Cover and simmer until daikon is tender, about 10 to 15 minutes.

6. Add the remaining ingredients except rice flour and oil. Cover and simmer for 10 minutes. Cool to room temperature.

7. Stir rice flour into the daikon mixture. Blend thoroughly.

8. Oil sides and bottom of 8-inch-square Pyrex cake dish.

9. Spoon mixture into dish in a flat layer. Use a wet spatula to smooth top.

10. Fill wok with water to 1 inch below the round perforated tray. Cover with wok cover and bring water to rapid boil. The turnip mixture will be steamed for 1 hour, which means that you will need to refill wok with water several times. A good alternative to the wok is to arrange a steamer on top of a large stockpot that can hold enough water to make refilling unnecessary.

11. Place dish on perforated tray, cover, and steam for 1 hour over rapidly boiling water. Keep reserve water boiling in tea kettle to refill wok periodically. The cake is done when a toothpick or bamboo skewer inserted into it comes out clean.

12. Cool to room temperature.

13. Invert cake onto cutting board and cut into 1- × 2-inch pieces. Note: We are cutting the turnip cake into comparatively small pieces to be eaten with the fingers. It is usually cut into 2- × 3-inch rectangles for sit-down deem sum luncheons.

14. Refrigerate if not frying immediately.

15. Just before serving, heat 2 tablespoons oil in frying pan and fry cakes until lightly brown and heated through. Serve with Soy Sauce–Szechuan Peppercorn Oil–Vinegar Dip.

To make 32

4 medium-sized dried Chinese black mushrooms
⅓ cup dried shrimp
¼ cup tepid water
1 Chinese pork sausage
1 pound Japanese daikon
1 cup Chicken Stock (page 116)
2 tablespoons minced scallion, white only
1 teaspoon salt
1 teaspoon sugar
⅛ teaspoon ground white pepper
1 tablespoon Shao Hsing wine or dry sherry
2 tablespoons lard
2 cups rice flour (not sweet rice flour)

2 tablespoons oil

Soy Sauce–Szechuan Peppercorn Oil– Vinegar Dip (page 115)

STUFFED BEAN CURD

Yeung tofu

With the popularity of Japanese food, most Westerners believe that tofu (soybean curd) originated in Japan. In fact, it is a Chinese creation; the first soybeans were harvested there more than 2,000 years ago. This recipe uses the Chinese "firm" tofu, which has been pressed more firmly than other varieties. It is consequently easier to stuff and also easier to fry, due to its lower water content. Nevertheless, the tofu is still fragile and needs careful handling.

1. Soak dried mushrooms in tepid water to cover for about 30 minutes, or until soft and pliable. When reconstituted, squeeze out excess water. Cut off and discard stems. Mince caps.

2. Prepare remaining stuffing ingredients. Mix all together thoroughly, until pasty. Refrigerate until ready to use.

3. Prepare bean curd sauce. Reserve.

4. Cut each bean curd diagonally across.

5. Cradle a triangle in your palm and scoop out a pocket (about 1 tablespoon) along the cut side. Repeat with remaining tofu.

6. Dust each cavity and cut surface with cornstarch.

7. Fill each cavity with stuffing mixture, mounding it up to cover the cut surface. A damp spatula and/or fingers are helpful for this.

8. Heat a large heavy frying pan to hot, and coat the bottom with ¼ cup oil.

9. Place the triangles, filling side down, in the pan to fry at medium heat.

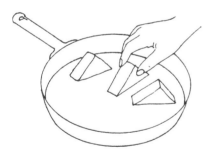

10. When filled edge is brown (about 4 minutes), turn the triangles on their flat sides.

11. Pour reserved bean curd sauce over tofu. Cover and simmer for 8 to 10 minutes.

12. Transfer tofu to serving plate. Serve hot with Mustard–Soy Sauce Dip.

To make 16

Stuffing:
2 dried black Chinese
  mushrooms
2 ounces shrimp,
  shelled, deveined, and
  rinsed
4 ounces ground pork,
  finely minced
½ egg, beaten
1 tablespoon minced
  coriander
1 tablespoon minced
  scallion, white part
½ teaspoon finely
  minced ginger
2 teaspoons tapioca
  starch
2 teaspoons Shao Hsing
  wine or dry sherry
1½ teaspoons soy sauce
1 teaspoon sugar
⅛ teaspoon salt
½ teaspoon sesame oil
Dash ground white
  pepper
1 tablespoon Chicken
  Stock (page 116)
1 tablespoon oyster
  sauce

Bean Curd Sauce (page
  115)
8 cakes firm Chinese
  bean curd
Cornstarch for dusting
Oil for pan-frying

Mustard–Soy Sauce Dip
  (page 115)

ROASTED OR BAKED DISHES

BARBECUED PORK

Char shiu

One of the great pleasures of exploring foreign cuisines is discovering totally different approaches to cooking the same thing. This "barbecued" pork recipe (which is not barbecued, but oven-roasted) is just such a tasty departure from familiar flavors. When cut into bite-size pieces, barbecued pork makes a delicious appetizer. But it has numerous other uses. It is the basis for the pork bun filling, a few pieces are usually tossed into noodle dishes, it can be cooked with vegetables, and so on. Keep a handy supply in your freezer.

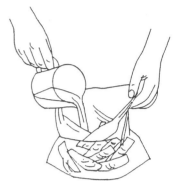

1. Cut the pork into 1- × 2-inch strips with the grain. Place in a large, sealable plastic bag.

2. Mix marinade and pour it into the bag. Mix well, seal, and refrigerate overnight.

3. Slide one oven rack into the topmost position and another into the lowest position in your oven. Place a large baking pan filled with ½ inch of water on the lower oven rack.

4. Preheat the oven to 450°F.

5. Combine glaze ingredients in a small saucepan and add 1 tablespoon marinade. Bring to a boil and turn heat off.

6. Attach a drapery hook to the end of each strip of meat.

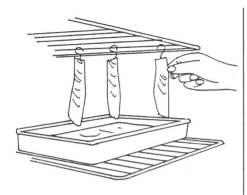

7. Hang the strips in the oven from the upper rack. Sliding rack partially out will make this easier. The Chinese method is to hang the meat in this manner to allow full hot air circulation. The strips may also be laid (well separated) on an oiled rack in the center of the oven for approximately the same result.

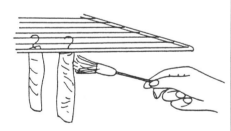

8. Roast the meat for 20 minutes at 450°F. and then reduce heat to 350°F. Roast for an additional 30 minutes, brushing with glaze several times during this period.

9. Take the meat out and cool for 15 minutes.

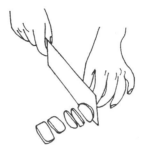

10. Slice meat into bite-size slices. Arrange the slices attractively on serving plate. May be served with hot mustard. Sprinkle toasted white sesame seeds over for added flavor.

Serves about 8

2 pounds pork loin

Marinade:
1 tablespoon minced
  ginger root
1 tablespoon minced
  garlic
¼ cup soy sauce
⅓ cup sugar
2 tablespoons Shao
  Hsing wine or dry
  sherry
1 tablespoon catsup
1 tablespoon hoisin
  sauce
1 tablespoon ground
  bean sauce
1 teaspoon five-spice
  powder

Glaze:
3 tablespoons honey
1 tablespoon soy sauce
1 teaspoon sesame oil

Special equipment:
Drapery hooks

GOLDEN COIN PORK

Gum cheen gai

This famous deem sum requires that the pork be marinated for about eight hours, so you have to start early—but the wait is worth it. The pork can be cooked in advance and refrigerated or frozen. The saltpeter in the marinade is used to give a lively reddish brown tone to the meat when cooked. It is optional but recommended for the otherwise drab, gray pork.

1. Slice pork into ¼-inch slices against the grain.

2. Prepare marinade.

3. Place the pork in a sealable plastic bag and pour marinade over. Mix well. Seal. Marinate, refrigerated, for 8 hours.

4. Prepare the golden pork bun dough.

5. Divide the dough in half. Place one half on a lightly floured board. Return other half to covered bowl.

6. Roll dough into cylinder about 2 inches in diameter.

7. Cut into about 15 1-inch pieces.

8. Cover the sections with a damp towel.

9. Flatten one section (cut sides up and down) between the palms.

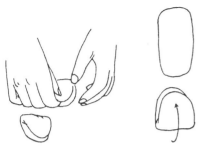

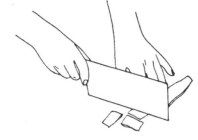

10. With a small rolling pin, roll out to a 2- × 5-inch rectangle. Fold over as shown to form an envelopelike bun.

11. Repeat with remaining ingredients and other half of dough. Set aside in oiled steamer compartments or on oiled baking pans until ready to steam. Cover with floured towel.

12. Preheat the oven to 300°F.

13. Prepare the glaze.

14. Spread the marinated pork slices on an oiled oven rack in a single layer and bake for 25 to 30 minutes.

15. Turn and brush with glaze every 5 minutes.

16. Remove and allow to cool to room temperature.

17. Cut the pork strips into small "coins" about 1 × 1½ inches.

18. Steam the pork buns for 20 minutes and serve them hot with the pork at room temperature. The buns may be served on one platter and the pork on another. Or several buns and a small quantity of pork may be served individually to each guest. Golden coin pork is eaten by opening a bun, inserting a few coins, and eating it sandwich-style.

To make 30

2 pounds pork loin

Marinade:
3 tablespoons Shao Hsing wine or dry sherry
6 tablespoons honey
2 tablespoons hoisin sauce
2 tablespoons ground bean sauce
¼ cup oyster sauce
¼ cup soy sauce
3 tablespoons sugar
¼ cup catsup
1 teaspoon saltpeter (optional)

30 golden coin pork buns (see Basic Bun Dough, page 104)

Glaze:
3 tablespoons honey
1 tablespoon water

BARBECUED SPARERIBS

Shiu pai gwut

For this recipe, it will be necessary to ask your butcher to cut the ribs into bite-size pieces. This is a job best left to him. Attacking the ribs with a cleaver at home is not a promising idea. Of course, the ribs may be left whole. Since we are using the smaller, more meaty backribs, you may prefer to serve them that way. Slightly different cooking times are noted in the recipe. Either way, they will be quickly snatched up, so make plenty.

1. Prepare the marinade ingredients and combine in a small bowl. Mix well.

2. Place the ribs in a sealable plastic bag and pour in marinade. Seal the bag, eliminating air. Knead the bag to circulate the marinade. Refrigerate for 8 hours.

3. Preheat the oven to 425°F.

4. Partially fill a shallow baking pan with water.

5. Oil a wire rack and fit it into the baking pan. (Water must not touch rack.)

6. Spread ribs meat side up on the rack, leaving space between each.

7. Prepare the glaze.

8. Place ribs in the upper third of the oven and bake for 10 minutes. Brush with glaze.

9. Reduce heat to 350°F. and bake for 5 minutes (whole rib, 20 minutes). Turn ribs and bake for 10 more minutes (whole rib, 15 to 20 minutes).

10. Brush with glaze. Return to oven for 3 more minutes to set. (If baking whole rib, brush glaze on meat side.)

11. Remove ribs from the oven. They may be served hot or cold. (Cut whole rib into individual ribs before serving.)

To make 50 to 60 pieces

Marinade:
2 tablespoons mashed fermented red bean curd (optional)
1 teaspoon minced ginger root
1 teaspoon minced garlic
1 tablespoon Shao Hsing wine or dry sherry
2 tablespoons catsup
3 tablespoons honey
2 tablespoons hoisin sauce
1 tablespoon ground bean sauce
2 tablespoons soy sauce
1 teaspoon five-spice powder
1 tablespoon sugar
1 teaspoon saltpeter (optional)

2 pounds backribs, cut into bite-size pieces

Glaze:
2 tablespoons honey
1 tablespoon water

CHICKEN TURNOVERS

Gai gok

The classic Western turnover is given a Chinese twist with a shredded chicken and black mushroom filling marinated in coriander, ginger juice, soy sauce, and Shao Hsing wine.

1. Soak dried mushrooms in tepid water to cover for about 30 minutes, or until soft and pliable. When reconstituted, squeeze out excess water, cut off and discard stems, and mince caps.

2. Prepare chicken and marinade. Place chicken and mushrooms in bowl. Pour marinade over and stir. Marinate for at least 2 hours.

3. Prepare pastry dough.

4. Heat ¼ cup oil in wok. Stir-fry onion until transparent. Add marinated chicken-mushroom mixture and stir-fry until just done. Reserve.

5. Combine sauce ingredients in a saucepan and cook over medium heat, stirring constantly, until sauce thickens. Stir in chicken-mushroom mixture and set aside to cool.

6. Preheat oven to 450°F.

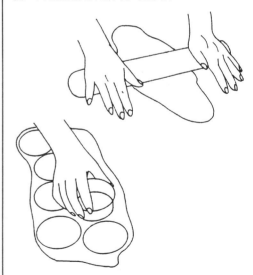

7. Roll out pastry dough to ⅛ inch thick. Using 3-inch-diameter round pastry cutter, cut out rounds.

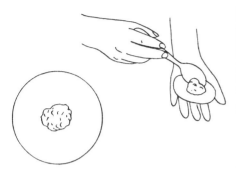

8. Place a tablespoon of filling on pastry round.

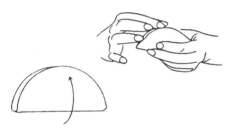

9. Fold over and pinch center.

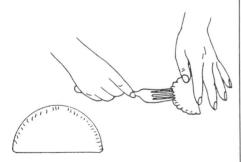

10. Press edges together. Press with fork tines for a decorative effect.

11. Prick center to allow steam to escape.

12. Repeat with remaining ingredients.

13. Place on ungreased baking sheet. Brush with egg and bake for 15 minutes, or until lightly browned.

To make 30

6 dried black Chinese mushrooms
1 whole chicken breast (about 1 pound) skinned, boned, and shredded

Marinade:
¼ cup minced coriander
½ teaspoon ginger juice
2 teaspoons light soy sauce
¼ teaspoon salt
½ teaspoon sugar
⅛ teaspoon white pepper
1 tablespoon Shao Hsing wine or dry sherry
1 tablespoon peanut oil
1 tablespoon cornstarch
½ egg white
1 teaspoon sesame oil

1 recipe Pastry Dough (page 106)

½ cup chopped onion
¼ cup oil

Sauce:
1 cup Chicken Stock (page 116)
2 teaspoons oyster sauce
2 teaspoons light soy sauce
1 teaspoon Shao Hsing wine or dry sherry
3 tablespoons cornstarch

1 egg, beaten

SWEET DISHES

CUSTARD TARTS

Daan tart

These tiny custard-filled tarts are traditional tea-house pastries. Long tradition, however, has not made them any easier to make. Pay careful attention to oven times and temperatures. An overly hot oven will cause the custard to collapse.

1. Sift together flour and salt.

2. Chop in butter and lard with pastry blender or knife to small pea size.

3. Mix beaten egg with ice water and add to flour mixture.

4. Gather by hand to form ball. Divide in half. Wrap each half in plastic wrap and refrigerate for 30 minutes.

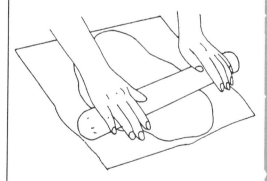

5. Lightly flour pastry cloth or board. Remove one portion of dough from refrigerator, place on pastry cloth, and roll out to ⅛-inch-thick sheet. Fold in thirds and roll out again. Repeat folding and rolling out several more times.

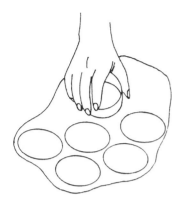

6. Flour the top lightly. Cut into disks with 3-inch-diameter cookie cutter.

7. Gather up remnants and set aside.

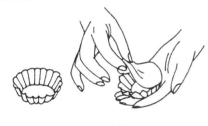

8. Place pastry disk, floured side down, into 2½-inch tartlet tin. Use chopstick to push the dough into the sides of the tin. Repeat with remaining pastry disks.

9. Roll out remaining dough and remnants and repeat procedure until all of tartlet tins are lined with dough.

10. Preheat oven to 400°F.

11. Beat eggs and egg yolks until thoroughly blended.

12. Add sugar, salt, half-and-half, and vanilla and stir until smooth and sugar dissolves. Pour the mixture into pastry lined tartlet tins, filling ¾ full.

13. Place the filled tins on cookie sheet and bake 7 minutes. Reduce temperature to 300°F. and bake until knifepoint inserted in center comes out almost clean, about 4 minutes longer. Custard continues to cook after removal from oven, so do not overbake.

14. Remove and cool (off cookie sheet) for about 30 minutes.

15. Remove from tins (by inverting) and serve.

To make 30

Pastry:
1¾ cups all-purpose flour
¼ teaspoon salt
¼ cup unsalted butter, diced and chilled
½ cup lard, diced and chilled.
1 egg, lightly beaten
2 tablespoons ice water

Filling:
3 large eggs plus 2 egg yolks, at room temperature
⅔ cup sugar
½ teaspoon salt
1½ cups half-and-half, at room temperature
1 teaspoon vanilla

Thirty 2½-inch tartlet tins

SESAME SEED BALLS

Jeen duey

These little delights blend two different kinds of subtle sweetness—that of the sweet rice dough exterior and the red bean interior filling. They are given a crunchy surface by coating with sesame seeds and deep-frying. Fry just prior to serving for superlative flavor.

1. Prepare sweet rice dough and refrigerate it.

2. Wash beans in cold water. Discard any that float.

3. Put beans in a 2-quart pan. Add 3 cups water and bring to boil, uncovered, over high heat.

4. When water boils, add ½ cup more water and reduce heat to medium. Cook, covered, until beans are tender enough to be easily mashed between thumb and forefinger, about 2 hours. Replace water as necessary to keep beans covered. Cool in liquid to room temperature.

5. Place beans and liquid in work bowl of food processor with metal blade. Purée.

6. Place towel in mixing bowl. Pour in beans. Gather four corners together and twist to squeeze out excess liquid. Discard liquid.

7. Toast black sesame seeds and pulverize in food processor or blender. Set aside.

8. Heat lard in wok over medium heat until liquefied. Add bean paste, sugar, and salt. Cook over medium heat while stirring constantly until beans are the consistency of slightly dry mashed potatoes, about 25 minutes. Careful—the mixture burns easily.

9. Stir in pulverized black sesame seeds. The mixture should be very thick at this point.

10. Place in shallow bowl and cool to room temperature.

11. Divide into 40 portions. Roll each into a ball. Cover and set aside.

12. Remove dough from the refrigerator and divide in half. Rewrap one half and set aside. Knead other portion a few times. Form into cylinder 1 inch in diameter.

13. Cut into 20 sections and form each section into a ball. Cover with damp cloth. Repeat with other portion.

14. Take 1 dough ball and form into shallow cup.

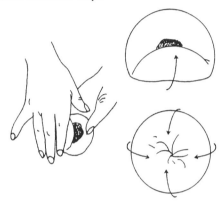

15. Insert a bean paste ball in the dough cup. Bring up sides to close opening and roll in palm to form even ball. Set aside under damp cloth. Repeat with remaining dough and bean paste.

16. Roll formed balls in white sesame seeds to coat.

17. Heat 4 to 6 cups of oil in wok to 360°F.

18. Deep-fry balls for about 1½ minutes. Remove when each floats. Serve hot.

To make 40

Sweet Rice Dough (page 108)

Filling:
8 ounces dried red beans
¼ cup black sesame seeds, toasted
½ cup lard
1¼ cups sugar
½ teaspoon salt

½ cup white sesame seeds
Oil for deep-frying

BLACK SESAME ROLLS

Jee ma guen

We have saved the black sesame roll for last. It is certainly the most unusual dessert in the deem sum repertoire. Its shiny, distinctive blackness and mildly sweet sesame flavor will make for an exciting finale to your deem sum feast.

1. Dry-toast sesame seeds over low heat until fragrant. Quickly empty into small blender jar. Set blender to blend and process for 5 minutes, occasionally stopping to scrape sides. Add corn oil and set machine to purée. Process 5 minutes or until mixture resembles soft peanut butter. Stop to scrape sides occasionally.

2. Put sesame seed paste in the processor work bowl with 1 cup water. Process until paste dissolves completely. Add remaining water, sugar, water chestnut powder, and cornstarch. Process until blended. Pour into large bowl.

3. Heat water in steamer.

4. Lightly oil shallow cake pan. Set aside.

5. Oil bottom and sides of 2 heavy-duty cake pans. (Avoid light aluminum pans; heat will distort these. An absolutely flat bottom is essential.)

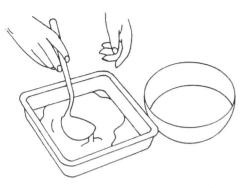

6. Stir batter well. Pour ½ cup into first heavy-duty cake pan.

7. Set pan level in hot steamer and steam for 4 minutes. Remove and set aside to cool.

8. Stir batter again and repeat with second heavy-duty pan.

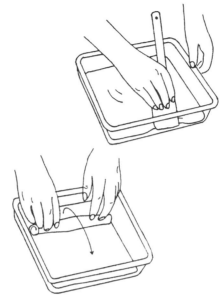

9. Loosen sides with spatula and gently begin to roll up sheet.

10. Remove and place on reserved oiled cake pan, seam side down.

11. Repeat with remaining batter, stirring batter and oiling pan each time.

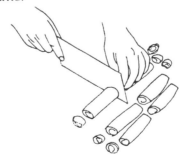

12. To serve, trim ½ inch from each end of roll and cut remainder in half. Serve at room temperature. If you refrigerate, resteam the rolls for a few minutes (until they soften) before serving.

To make 10 rolls

⅔ cup black sesame
   seeds
2 tablespoons corn oil
3 cups water
1½ cups sugar
½ cup water chestnut
   powder
½ cup cornstarch

Oil for pans

DOUGHS

HAR GOW DOUGH

Har gow pay

Har gow dough turns translucent when steamed, allowing the contents of the dumpling, usually a savory shrimp mixture, to show through—a temptation seldom resisted. The dough can be difficult to handle since wheat starch lacks the gluten that makes doughs adhesive. But learning to use this dough is one of the great rewards of practicing deem sum cookery.

1. Sift wheat starch and tapioca starch together into a bowl.

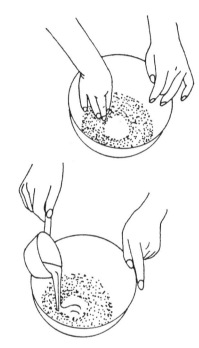

2. Form a cavity in center of starch mixture. Quickly pour in boiling water and vigorously stir into a ball. This cooks the starches, which results in a transparent wrapper. It is important not to let the water cool. (A microwave oven is useful for boiling a small, exact amount of water.)

3. Add lard and knead until well blended. (A blender does not seem to work well with small amounts of wheat starch. Hand mixing gives the best results.)

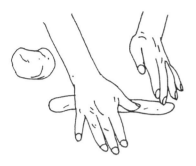

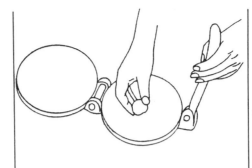

To make about 30

1½ cups wheat starch
2 tablespoons tapioca
  starch
1 cup boiling water
1 tablespoon lard

Oil for tortilla press

Special equipment:
Tortilla press, Chinese
  cleaver, or small
  rolling pin

4. Divide ball in two. Roll each half into 1-inch-diameter cylinder.

5. Cover with damp towel and let rest for 15 minutes.

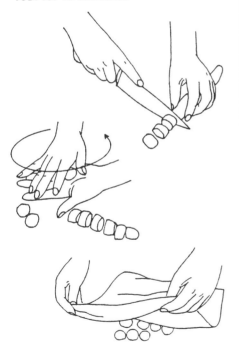

7. Oil both sides of a tortilla press. Press the balls into thin wafers of diameter required by recipe. Re-oil the press as necessary. Chinese chefs will press out the wafers by using the oiled side of a cleaver against a flat, oiled surface. A small rolling pin is slower, but will also work.

6. Slice each cylinder into ¾-inch pieces, roll into balls, and cover with damp towel. Keep in this form until ready to use.

POT STICKER WRAPPERS

War teep pay

These wrappers are made with a conventional flour dough. It turns a slightly tan color when cooked rather than the pure white of the preceding har gow dough. It is much easier to form into dumplings. Unfortunately, the wrappers are not readily available in stores. Commercial wonton wrappers (cut to 2½-inch circles) may be substituted, but they are thinner and the ingredients are different.

1. Put flour and salt in the processor bowl with metal blade attached. Affix cover.

2. Turn the motor on and slowly begin adding water through the food chute until dough forms into a loose ball around the blade. (You may not need all the water.)

3. Place dough on a lightly floured surface and knead for about 30 seconds.

4. Shape into ball and place in bowl covered with plastic wrap for 30 minutes at room temperature.

5. Place dough on lightly floured surface. Divide into thirds. Return two-thirds to bowl and cover with damp cloth.

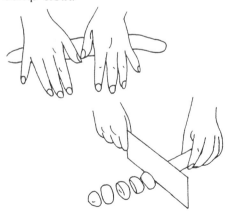

6. Roll remaining third into cylinder about 12 inches long and 1 inch in diameter. Cut into 1-inch pieces.

7. Place a piece of dough between hands with cut sides against each palm. Squeeze flat.

8. Using a small rolling pin, roll dough out to 2½-inch diameter. (Proper war teep pay wrappers have thicker centers than edges. A small rolling pin, tapered toward the ends, achieves this. The tapered ends create a thicker center when rolling out in a circular fashion.)

9. Repeat with the remaining dough. Place wrappers on a floured plate and cover with a damp towel until ready to use.

To make about 36

3 cups all-purpose flour
½ teaspoon salt
1 cup tepid water

BASIC BUN DOUGH

Bow pay

Basic bun dough is used in this book for barbecued pork buns and for golden coin pork. The dough ingredients are the same. For the pork bun, the dough is formed into a ball around the filling and then steamed. The dough for golden coin pork is formed into a pocket and steamed first. The pork filling is then added by each guest and eaten like a sandwich. This recipe will make 24 pork buns or 30 or more golden coin buns. Speaking of sandwiches, golden coin buns make delicious, different sandwich buns for light luncheons or buffets.

1. Check to make sure yeast is active by sprinkling it over ½ cup of tepid water. Let stand until completely dissolved and the mixture begins to bubble, about 5 minutes.

2. Mix flour, sugar, and salt together by hand in a large bowl.

3. Add softened lard, the dissolved yeast, milk, and remaining water. Mix with wooden spoon.

4. Turn out dough onto a lightly floured board. Add baking powder and knead until it becomes smooth and loses most of its stickiness. (Basic bun dough may be made in a food processor with the metal blade attached. Mix dry ingredients together in the work bowl. Add lard, dissolved yeast mixture, water, and milk through the feed tube with the machine running. Process until a moist, elastic ball is formed, about 1 minute. Adjust the consistency by adding more flour or water. Do this in two parts.)

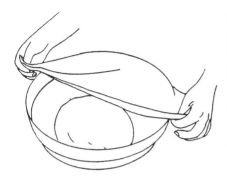

5. Place the dough ball in a large oiled ceramic bowl and cover with a damp towel. (A metal bowl does not insulate well enough.)

6. Warm oven at lowest temperature setting for 2 minutes and then turn off.

7. Place the covered dough in the oven for 1 hour or until double in volume. The dough is now ready to be shaped as required by the recipe.

To make 25 to 30

1 package dry yeast
1¼ cups tepid water
6 cups all-purpose flour
⅓ cup sugar
½ teaspoon salt
3 tablespoons lard, softened at room temperature
½ cup milk
2 teaspoons baking powder

PASTRY DOUGH

So pay

Certain deem sum require a conventional flaky pastry dough such as the one below. It is the traditional two-part dough used for pie crusts and turnovers.

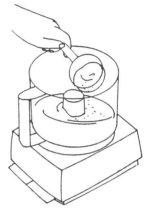

1. To prepare dough "A": Affix metal blade in food processor. Put flour, sugar, and salt into bowl, cover, and process for 3 seconds.

2. With machine running, add lard rapidly through feed tube and process 3 seconds.

3. Add egg yolks and water. Process another 3 seconds, or until dough starts to form. Stop.

4. Remove dough from processor and form into two equal balls. Wrap separately in plastic wrap. Refrigerate for 30 minutes.

5. To prepare dough "B": Put flour into processor bowl. With machine on, add lard rapidly through the feed tube and process until granular in appearance, about 4 seconds.

6. Remove and form two equal balls. Wrap separately in plastic and refrigerate for 30 minutes.

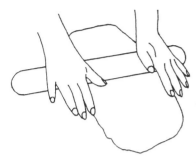

7. On a lightly floured surface, roll out one of the dough "A" balls to a 9-by 12-inch rectangle.

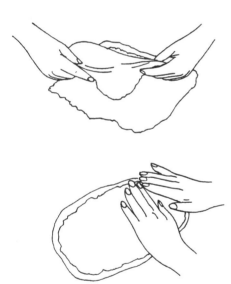

8. Roll out a dough "B" ball to a slightly smaller size.

9. Place the dough "B" sheet on top of dough "A." Fold in thirds. Re-flour board surface and roll out to ⅛-inch thickness.

10. Repeat procedure with remaining dough.

To make about 30 three-inch wafers

Dough "A":
1¼ cups all-purpose flour
2 teaspoons sugar
¼ teaspoon salt
4 tablespoons chilled lard cut into ½-inch pieces
2 large egg yolks
¼ cup ice water

Dough "B":
1¼ cups all-purpose flour
6 tablespoons chilled lard cut into ½-inch pieces

SWEET RICE DOUGH

Haam suey gok pay

Sweet rice flour becomes sticky when cooked. It lends a unique sweetness and texture to the dough. Pastries made with sweet rice dough are definitely one of the addictive pleasures of deem sum cookery.

1. Put sweet rice flour in a bowl and mix in ¾ cup water. Mix by hand until it forms into a dough. Set aside.

2. In another bowl, add softened lard to wheat starch and mix together.

3. Add brown sugar to ⅔ cup water and stir until dissolved. Bring water to boil and pour into wheat starch mixture while stirring vigorously.

4. Add the wheat starch mixture to bowl of sweet rice flour and mix well by hand.

5. Turn out on lightly floured surface and knead until thoroughly mixed, about 10 minutes.

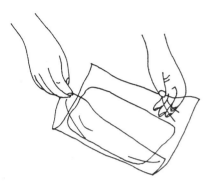

6. Flatten the dough to ½ inch in thickness and wrap with plastic wrap. Refrigerate for 1½ hours.

2 cups sweet rice flour
¾ cup water
¼ cup lard, softened
⅔ cup wheat starch
¼ cup dark brown
  sugar, packed
⅔ cup boiling water

WONTON SKINS

Wun tun pay

Wonton skins can be either purchased commercially or made at home. Since home recipes are richer and tastier and the process isn't difficult, we recommend that you try. A conventional manual pasta machine is used to roll the dough into thin sheets from which the 2½-inch squares are cut.

1. Mix the flour, egg, and salt until it can be formed into a ball.

2. On a lightly floured work surface, knead the dough until smooth and stiff, about 10 minutes.

3. Divide dough into 4 equal parts, wrap each with plastic wrap, and set aside for 30 minutes.

4. Press 1 part into a flat rectangle.

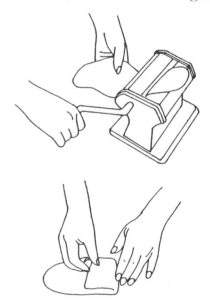

5. Adjust pasta machine dial to widest setting. Run dough through once. Fold in thirds and repeat at same setting. Repeat 5 times. Sprinkle lightly with flour if necessary to prevent sticking but do not over-flour. Do not fold dough on last run-through.

6. Continue to run dough through pasta machine, adjusting to thinner setting each time. Continue to thinnest setting that permits dough through without tearing.

7. Lay long strip of dough on work surface and sprinkle with cornstarch.

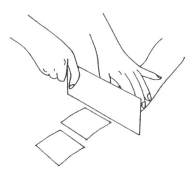

8. Cut dough into approximately 25 two and one-half inch squares. Stack and wrap with plastic.

9. Repeat with remaining dough and remnants.

10. Wonton skins may be frozen for up to one month if wrapped airtight.

To make about 100

2 cups all-purpose flour
3 large eggs
1 teaspoon salt

cornstarch for dusting

OILS, SAUCES, AND STOCK

SZECHUAN PEPPERCORN OIL

½ cup corn oil
3 tablespoons Szechuan peppercorns

1. Heat oil over high heat.

2. Add peppercorns and immediately turn heat off.

3. Let stand for 2 minutes.

4. Strain out peppercorns and discard.

5. Store oil in tightly sealed bottle. It will keep indefinitely if refrigerated.

CHILI PEPPER OIL

4 scallions
1 large fresh ginger root, unpeeled
2 cups corn oil
⅓ cup dried chili pepper flakes

1. Cut each scallion into 3-inch lengths.

2. Smash ginger root with side of cleaver.

3. Heat oil in wok over high heat. Add scallions and ginger. Turn heat off immediately. After 5 minutes, discard scallions and ginger. Cool for 5 more minutes.

4. Place chili flakes in a bowl and ladle cooled oil over them. Cover and leave overnight at room temperature. Strain oil and bottle it. Store the chili flakes in a covered jar. Both will keep indefinitely if refrigerated.

SOY SAUCE–CHILI PEPPER OIL DIP

½ cup soy sauce
3 tablespoons Chili Pepper Oil (see above)

1. Soy sauce and chili pepper oil may be mixed in advance in these proportions, or separate containers of soy sauce and chili pepper oil may be provided to be mixed to taste by guests.

SOY SAUCE–CHILI PEPPER OIL–VINEGAR DIP

½ cup soy sauce
2 teaspoons (or to taste) Chili Pepper Oil (see above)
3 tablespoons rice vinegar
2 teaspoons dark brown sugar

1. Combine all ingredients and mix until sugar dissolves.

SOY SAUCE–SZECHUAN PEPPERCORN OIL DIP

½ cup soy sauce
2 tablespoons Szechuan Peppercorn Oil (page 114)

1. Combine ingredients in these proportions or serve separately to be combined by each guest to taste.

MUSTARD–SOY SAUCE DIP

1 tablespoon Coleman's mustard powder
1½ teaspoons cold water
½ cup soy sauce

1. Put mustard powder in a small cup. Add cold water and mix vigorously with chopstick. Cover and let stand 10 minutes.

2. Serve with soy sauce to be mixed together to taste by each guest.

SOY SAUCE–SZECHUAN PEPPERCORN OIL–VINEGAR DIP

⅓ cup soy sauce
¼ cup Szechuan Peppercorn Oil (page 114)
3 tablespoons rice vinegar

1. Ingredients may be mixed together in the above proportions, or provided separately to be mixed to taste by each guest.

BEAN CURD SAUCE

1½ tablespoons oyster sauce
1½ teaspoons sugar
¼ teaspoon salt
dash pepper
½ teaspoon sesame oil
¾ cup Chicken Stock (page 116)
1 tablespoon Shao Hsing wine or dry sherry

2 teaspoons cornstarch mixed with 1 tablespoon
    water

1. Combine sauce ingredients (except cornstarch-water mixture) in a small saucepan. Bring to a simmer.

2. Stir in cornstarch-water mixture.

3. Simmer while stirring until sauce thickens slightly.

CHICKEN STOCK

The following recipe for chicken stock is always used in this book. If canned chicken stock is used instead, the results are often too salty unless salt is reduced or eliminated in the main recipe.

To make 6 cups

4 chicken backs, about 2½ pounds
3 scallions, crushed

1. Cut backs in half. Place in 5-quart pan and add water to cover completely.

2. Bring to simmer. Skim as necessary.

3. Simmer for 20 minutes. Add scallions.

4. Partially cover pot, leaving about 1 inch open.

5. Simmer slowly for 4 hours. Do not allow it to boil, which will cloud liquid.

6. Turn heat off. Remove as much of the scallions, bones, and meat as possible. Set aside for 10 minutes to settle. Spoon off fat. Cool to room temperature.

7. Strain through fine sieve. If stock needs to be degreased further, place in refrigerator, uncovered, overnight. Fat will congeal on surface for easy removal.

8. Store by freezing in small containers. To make stock cubes pour ¼ cup stock into each section of ice cube tray and freeze. Remove and store frozen stock cubes in plastic freezer bag.

9. If stock is stored unfrozen in refrigerator, it must be reboiled for a couple of minutes every 3 or 4 days to keep from spoiling.

INDEX

Baked dishes, *see* Roasted or baked dishes
Bamboo shoots, 3
Bamboo steamer, 12–13
Barbecued Pork, 82–83
Barbecued Pork Buns, 28–29
Barbecued Spareribs, 86–87
Basic Bun Dough, 104–105
    Barbecued Pork Buns, 28–29
    Golden Coin Pork, 84–85
Baw pay, 104–105
Bean curd (red), 3
Bean curd (tofu), 3
    Stuffed, 78–79
Bean Curd Sauce, 115
Bean Curd Skin Rolls, 60–63
Bean curd skins, 3
    Bean Curd Skin Rolls, 60–63
Bean sauce, 3
Beef:
    Baskets, 22–23
    Rice Noodle Roll, 36–37
    and Watercress, 30–31
Black beans, 3
Black Chinese mushrooms, *see* Mushrooms, black Chinese
Black Sesame Rolls, 96–97
Black sesame seeds, *see* Sesame seeds, black
Bread, white, for Shrimp Toast, 48–49

Cabbage, Chinese, 4
    Pot Stickers, 74–75
Char Shiu, 82–83
Char shiu bow, 28–29

"Cheese" Wun tun, 68–69
Cheung fun, 36–37
Cheun guen, 52–55
Chicken:
    Crescents, 20–21
    Lollipops, 50–51
    Lotus Leaf Rice, 40–43
    Silver Wrapped, 66–67
    Stock, 4, 116
    Turnovers, 88–89
Chili oil, 4
Chili Pepper Oil, 114
    Dip, Soy Sauce/, 114
    Soy Sauce/Vinegar Dip, 114
Chili peppers, 4
Chili pepper sauce, 4
Chinese cabbage, *see* Cabbage, Chinese
Chinese pork sausage, *see* Sausage, Chinese pork
Chives, Chinese, 5
Chopsticks, long, cooking, 15, 18
Coriander, 4–5
Crabmeat, Stuffed Crab Claws, 70–71
Cream Cheese Wonton, 68–69
Custard Tarts, 92–93

Daan tart, 92–93
Daikon (Chinese turnip), 5
    Turnip Cakes, 76–77
Deem sum, tradition of, 1–2
Deep-fried dishes, 48–71
    Bean Curd Skin Rolls, 60–63
    Chicken Lollipops, 50–51

Cream Cheese Wonton, 68–69
Fried Fish Balls, 64–65
Shrimp Toast, 48–49
Silver Wrapped Chicken, 66–67
Spring Rolls, 52–55
Stuffed Crab Claws, 70–71
Sweet Rice Dumplings, 58–59
Taro Dumplings, 46–47
Deep-frying, 14–18
Dip:
    Mustard/Soy Sauce, 115
    Soy Sauce/Chili Pepper Oil, 114
    Soy Sauce/Chili Pepper Oil/Vinegar, 114
    Soy Sauce/Szechuan Peppercorn Oil, 115
    Soy Sauce/Szechuan Peppercorn Oil/Vinegar, 115
Double-frying, 18
Duck eggs (preserved), 5
Doughs, 100–11
    Basic Bun Dough, 104–105
    Har Gow Dough, 100–101
    Pastry Dough, 106–107
    Pot Sticker Wrappers, 102–103
    Sweet Rice Dough, 108–109
    Wonton Skins, 110–11

Egg roll skins, 5
Eggs for Custard Tarts, 92–93

Fish Balls, Fried, 64–65
Five-spice powder, 5

Four Color Dumplings, 24—25
Fried Fish Balls, 64—65

Gai gok, 88—89
Gai nup fun gwor, 20—21
Ginger root, 5
Glutinous rice, 6
    Lotus Leaf Rice, 40—43
    Steamed Pearl Balls, 38—39
Gnow yuk shiu mye, 22—23
Gum cheen gai, 84—85
Gum yue gow, 44—45

Haam suey gok, 58—59
Haam suey gok pay, 108—109
Har dor see, 48—49
Har gow, 26—27
Har Gow Dough, 100—101
    Chicken Crescents, 20—21
    Mandarin Dumplings, 34—35
    Shrimp Goldfish, 44—45
    Shrimp Moons, 26—27
Har gow pay, 100—101
Hoison sauce, 5

Ingredients, 3—8

Jar yue yuen, 64—65
Jee bow gai, 66—67
Jee ma guen, 96—97
Jeen duey, 94—95
Jun jew kao, 38—39

Ladle, 9
Lard, 5
Law bak go, 76—77
Lotus Leaf Rice, 40—43
Lotus leaves (dried), 5
    Lotus Leaf Rice, 40—43

Mandarin Dumplings, 34—35

Metal steamer, 11—12
Mushrooms, black Chinese, 3—4
    Bean Curd Skin Rolls, 60—63
    Chicken Turnovers, 88—89
    Four Color Dumplings, 24—25
Mustard (hot), 5—6
Mustard/Soy Sauce Dip, 115

Naw mai gai, 40—43

Oil:
    Chili Pepper, 114
    for deep-frying, 14—15
    Soy Sauce/Chili Pepper Oil
        Dip, 114
    Soy Sauce/Chili Pepper Oil/
        Vinegar Dip, 114
    Soy Sauce/Szechuan Pepper-
        corn Oil Dip, 115
    Soy Sauce/Szechuan Pepper-
        corn Oil/Vinegar Dip, 115
    Szechuan Peppercorn, 114
Oyster sauce, 6
    Bean Curd Sauce, 115

Pan-fried dishes, 74—79
    Pot Stickers, 74—75
    Stuffed Bean Curd, 78—79
    Turnip Cakes, 76—77
Pastry Dough, 106—107
    Chicken Turnovers, 88—89
Pepper, see Szechuan pepper
Plum sauce, 6
Peanut oil, 14
Pork:
    Barbecued, 82—83
    Barbecued Spareribs, 86—87
    Bean Curd Skin Rolls, 60—63
    Buns, Barbecued, 28—29
    Four Color Dumplings, 24—25

Golden Coin, 84—85
Lotus Leaf Rice, 40—43
Pot Stickers, 74—75
sausages, see Sausages, Chi-
    nese pork
Spring Rolls, 52—55
Steamed Pearl Balls, 38—39
Steamed Spareribs, 32—33
Stuffed Bean Curd, 78—79
Sweet Rice Dumplings, 58—
    59
Taro Dumplings, 56—57
Pot Stickers, 74—75
Pot Sticker Wrappers, 102—103

Red bean paste, 6
Red beans, 6
    Sesame Seed Balls, 94—95
Rice, see Glutinous rice
Rice flour, 6
    glutinous, 6
    Turnip Cakes, 76—77
Rice Noodle Roll, 36—37
Roasted or baked dishes, 82—
    89
    Barbecued Pork, 82—83
    Barbecued Spareribs, 86—87
    Chicken Turnovers, 88—89
    Golden Coin Pork, 84—85

Saam ling gow, 34—35
Safety, 15
Sai choy ngow yuk, 30—31
Saltpeter, 6
San juk guen, 60—63
Sausages, Chinese pork, 4
    Lotus Leaf Rice, 40—43
    Turnip Cakes, 76—77
Say sik shiu mye, 24—25
Screen circular metal, 15
Sesame oil, 6

Sesame seed paste, 7
Sesame seeds, black, 6–7
  Black Sesame Rolls, 96–97
  Sesame Seed Balls, 94–95
Shao Hsing wine, 7
Shiu mye wrappers, 7
  Beef Baskets, 22–23
  Four Color Dumplings, 24–25
Shrimp:
  Bean Curd Skin Rolls, 60–63
  dried, 7
  Goldfish, 44–45
  Mandarin Dumplings, 34–35
  Moons, 26–27
  Spring Rolls, 52–55
  Stuffed Crab Claws, 70–71
  Taro Dumplings, 56–57
  Toast, 48–49
  Turnip Cakes, 76–77
Silver Wrapped Chicken, 66–67
So pay, 106–107
Soy sauce, 7
  /Chili Pepper Oil Dip, 114
  /Chili Pepper Oil/Vinegar Dip, 114
  Dip, Mustard/, 115
  /Szechuan Peppercorn Oil Dip, 115
  /Szechuan Peppercorn Oil/ Vinegar Dip, 115
Spareribs:
  Barbecued, 86–87
  Steamed, 32–33
Spatula, 9
Spring Rolls, 52–55
Spring roll skins, 7
  Spring Rolls, 52–55
Stir-frying, 9–10

Steamed Pearl Balls, 38–39
Steamed dishes, 20–45
  Barbecued Pork Buns, 28–29
  Beef and Watercress, 30–31
  Beef Baskets, 22–23
  Chicken Crescents, 20–21
  Four Color Dumplings, 24–25
  Lotus Leaf Rice, 40–43
  Mandarin Dumplings, 34–35
  Rice Noodle Roll, 36–37
  Shrimp Goldfish, 44–45
  Shrimp Moons, 26–27
  Steamed Pearl Balls, 38–39
  Steamed Spareribs, 32–33
Steamed Spareribs, 32–33
Steamer, 10–13
  bamboo, 12–13
  metal, 11–12
Steaming, 10–14
Stock, Chicken, 4, 116
Strainer, Chinese mesh, 15, 17–18
Stuffed Bean Curd, 78–79
Stuffed Crab Claws, 70–71
Sweet dishes, 92–97
  Black Sesame Rolls, 96–97
  Custard Tarts, 92–93
  Sesame Seed Balls, 94–95
Sweet Rice Dough, 108–109
  Sesame Seed Balls, 94–95
  Sweet Rice Dumplings, 58–59
Sweet Rice Dumplings, 58–59
Szechuan pepper, 7
  Soy Sauce/Szechuan Peppercorn Oil Dip, 115
  Soy Sauce/Szechuan Peppercorn Oil/Vinegar Dip, 115
  Szechuan Peppercorn Oil, 114

Tapioca starch, 7
Taro Dumplings, 56–57
Taro root, 7
Techniques, 9–18
  deep-frying, 14–18
  steaming, 10–14
  stir-frying, 9–10
Thermometer, cooking, 17
Tofu, see Bean curd (tofu)
Tongs, 18
Tools and techniques, 9–18
Turnip Cakes, 76–77

Vinegar Dip:
  Soy Sauce/Chili Pepper Oil, 114
  Soy Sauce/Szechuan Peppercorn Oil/, 115

War teep, 74–75
War teep pay, 102–103
Water chestnut powder, 8
Water chestnuts, 7–8
Watercress, Beef and, 30–31
Wheat starch, 8
Wok, 9, 15–16
Wok burner, 16–17
Wonton skins, 8, 10–11
  Beef Baskets, 22–23
  Cream Cheese Wonton, 68–69
Woo gok, 56–57
Wun tun pay, 110–11

Yeung gai yik, 50–51
Yeung tofu, 78–79
Yick Company, Robert, 16